The Somerset & Dorset Railway

Opening of the Bath Extension 1874

Compiled *by*
Duncan Harper

and published *by*
Millstream Books
in a *limited edition* of 1,000
of which this copy is number
728

No. 165

In Parliament—Session 1865-6.

BRISTOL AND NORTH SOMERSET RAILWAY.

(SOUTHERN EXTENSION.)

1st December, 1865.

SIR,

We beg to inform you that application is intended to be made to Parliament in the ensuing Session for an Act to authorise (amongst other things) the making of Railways between the Bristol and North Somerset Railway at or near Farrington Gourney and the Somerset and Dorset Railway at or near Evercreech, with Branches therefrom to the East Somerset Railway at Shepton Mallet, and through the Nettlebridge Valley to the Frome and Radstock Branch of the Wilts, Somerset, and Weymouth Railway, and that the property mentioned in the annexed Schedule, or some part thereof, in which we understand you are interested as therein stated, will be required for the purposes of the said undertaking, according to the line thereof as at present laid out, or may be required to be taken under the usual powers of deviation on either side of the said line which will be applied for in the said Act; and that such property will be passed through in the manner mentioned in such Schedule.

We also beg to inform you, that a Plan and Section of the said undertaking, with a Book of Reference thereto, were deposited with the Clerk of the Peace for the County of Somerset, on or before the 30th of November, 1865, and that copies of so much of the said Plan and Section as relate to the Parish in which your property is situate, with a Book of Reference thereto, have been deposited for public inspection with the Clerk of the said Parish at his residence, on or before the said 30th day of November, on which Plans your property is designated by the numbers set forth in the annexed Schedule.

As we are required to report to Parliament whether you assent to or dissent from the proposed undertaking, or whether you are neuter in respect thereto, you will oblige us by writing your answer of assent, dissent, or neutrality in the form left herewith, and returning the same with your signature, on or before the 20th day of December instant, and if there should be any error or misdescription in the annexed Schedule, we shall feel obliged by your informing us thereof at your earliest convenience, that we may correct the same without delay.

We are, Sir,

Your obedient Servants,

WILLIAM TOOGOOD,
16, Parliament Street
JOHN BINGHAM,

During the 1860s the Somerset & Dorset Railway was something of a rural backwater. This scheme of 1865, promoted by the Bristol & North Somerset Railway, was one of several proposing direct access from the S&D to the Somerset coalfield and the major port of Bristol.

INTRODUCTION

The Somerset & Dorset Railway was not a financial success. It was a single-track, cross-country railway that had come into being in 1862, as an amalgamation of the Somerset Central and Dorset Central Railways. It ran from the small Bristol Channel ports of Burnham and Highbridge, across the Somerset levels to Glastonbury and on, down through Dorset, to Wimborne where it gained access to the English Channel at Poole Harbour. Despite the pretension of being a Channel to Channel link, it was essentially an agricultural railway, tapping no major natural resources and linking no significant centres of commerce or population. The S&D carried farm produce towards London by way of Templecombe, and to South Wales by sea in exchange for coal and iron. It served the local communities, but it lacked any broader purpose in its connections with neighbouring railway companies. It was not destined to be a financially viable railway in its present form, and the company probably realised that in order to survive, it would have to build its way out of trouble.

Within months of the amalgamation, Robert Read, the company secretary, was turning his eyes north, towards the Somerset coalfield and the railway route centre at Bristol where abundant sources of traffic were within tantalising reach. Several plans were drawn up for a junction near the mid point of the railway, and a line which would force its way from there, over the formidable rampart of the Mendip hills, to the coalfield and beyond. They were bold and ambitious ideas.

Ten years later, after much financial scheming, the dream was becoming a reality. Blasted through Mendip limestone, tucked into winding, wooded valleys, came a railway that was to fill the S&D with renewed purpose – a link into the Midland Railway's narrow-gauge empire at Bath, offering safe passage through broad-gauge territory from the north of England to the south coast. With the prize of Somerset coal at its heart, it was a masterstroke that hammered several lethal nails into the coffin of Brunel's broad gauge. The quantity of traffic that began to travel over the line was enough to reveal the folly of its cheap and hurried construction as a single track railway. But, despite the inevitable misfortunes that were yet to befall the line (near bankruptcy, lack of adequate expenditure on track, locomotives and staff, and dreadful loss of life two years later), nevertheless the Bath Extension was *the* great achievement of the independent Somerset & Dorset Railway, and this is the story of its opening on 20th July 1874.

Forming the core of this book is an account by D.H.Gale, which was originally printed by *Keene's Bath Journal* Office in that city. It was written to celebrate the completion and opening of the new line that had been built in the short space of two years, over and through the Mendip hills from Evercreech to Bath. The heavily engineered extension was a branch of the company's original line from Burnham to Wimborne. However, the railway from Bath to the south coast immediately acquired main line status, and the Evercreech to Burnham section became the branch.

Gale's account seems to have been based on his personal experience of a journey over the line shortly before its opening, when the earthworks and structures were brand new and, in some cases, not entirely finished; goods facilities for instance seem to have been incomplete at that time. The line as originally built was a single track, and the bridges, viaducts and tunnels had been constructed accordingly. The deep gouges made by the contractors into the hills had revealed fascinating glimpses of the naked geological structure of the terrain, and the sinuous valleys of north-east Somerset had been newly strung with elegant arches of stone or brick. Gale wrote very convincingly of the appearance of the new railway in the Mendip landscape, where it was obviously seen as a picturesque addition rather than a disfiguring intrusion.

Sometimes, Gale's facts were a little awry. For example, in his original text he referred to the East Somerset line at Shepton Mallet as the Somerset and Wilts; Charlton Road viaduct, that remarkable structure which still strides across the eastern outskirts of Shepton Mallet, Gale curiously described as being located just north of Evercreech. Despite his lapses, the immediacy of much of the writing clearly confirms his first-hand experience of the journey which was apparently made on the footplate where he "had the benefit of the smoke and steam" in Combe Down tunnel, fortunately with no ill effect.

Another peculiarity of Gale's account is the rather convoluted writing, where subordinate clauses are layered and interlaced, and where punctuation and grammar are inconsistent; mid-Victorian journalese, I suppose it is. I have taken the liberty of altering any obvious errors and ironing out the worst of the unintelligible sentences, but I have left enough to keep the flavour and vivacity of the original.

The account was published in book form, as a *Tourists' Descriptive Guide to the Somerset and Dorset Railway*. The imprint was "BATH: PRINTED BY JAMES KEENE, JOURNAL OFFICE, 1874". It was published in a small pocket-sized format with an ornamented border around each page of dense text, and was not illustrated at all. This makes it, by today's standards, rather dry reading. It is also very difficult to obtain now.

Gale fleshed out the tale of his journey with cumbersome historical commentaries on various locations that the line approached, particularly Bath itself. He also described, though much more briefly, the rest of the railway, firstly the line through Glastonbury to Burnham and then the remainder of the route to Bournemouth. As Gale's enthusiasm was obviously for his trip over the Bath Extension, and as this was where he made particularly detailed observations of the newly built railway, I have omitted the Burnham and Bournemouth sections, and edited out what I choose to read as antiquarian padding.

However, included in this edition of Gale's work is his useful summary of the history of the Somerset & Dorset Railway, together with a detailed description of the line's primary raison d'être, the Somerset coalfield. I have also chosen to complement his work with extracts from several other sources.

The first of these, which originally appeared in *Keene's Bath Journal*, is a report published on 25th July 1874 of the first public train to run over the S&D Extension. The anonymous journalist presented a colourful account of the trip to Evercreech and back, and excerpts from it are here interspersed with Gale's. These are identified by being set in *italic type*.

The second source is the rival *Bath Chronicle and Herald*, whose edition of 23rd July 1874 contained its own report of the opening day. This described the line with a degree of detail which serves sometimes to clarify and at other times to amplify Gale. Quotations from this are set in **bold type**.

The difference in emphasis between the two newspapers is interesting. Whereas the *Chronicle* writer seems to have been determined to damn the railway at the very outset for its poor timekeeping, *Keene's Journal* was content to give the line its blessing and the benefit of the doubt, blaming late running connections for the S&D's shortcomings.

The third extract is a brief description of Clandown Colliery by Mrs L.Wheatcroft. Although her visit took place more than twenty years after Gale's journey, some of her jottings are included here because she presents a delightful, first-hand glimpse of the Radstock area, at a time when the Somerset coalfield and its associated railways were perhaps at their most active. Her article was published as one of a series of "Picturesque Village Rambles" in the *Bath & County Graphic* journal of May 1898, and here follows Gale's background notes on the history of the Somerset coalfield. This section is also set in *italic type*.

Fourthly, inserted at the appropriate points in the narrative, are the instructions issued to S&DR employees for the operation of the new line. These presumably date from the opening of the line and were pasted into the company's *Book of Rules and Regulations*. They are identified by being set in **sans serif typeface**.

Lastly, the text concludes with the transcript of an advertisement published in the *Bath Chronicle and Herald* on 6th August 1874. From this we can see that just three weeks after the line opened to the public, the contractor was already auctioning off his plant and equipment – a fascinating list of machinery and animals, which helps to illustrate the methods that had been used in building the Bath Extension.

I have confined my own annotations throughout to captions for the illustrations and to comments printed in square parentheses within the body of the text.

The survival of the Somerset & Dorset well into the second half of the 20th century was really quite remarkable, since, although many improvements had been made to the infrastructure and operating practices over the years, it had become by then something of an anachronism. It was still essentially a Victorian railway. Analysing the appeal that the line has today would be a complex task, but surely one of the S&D's most endearing features in its last years was, simply, its dogged endurance in the face of the modern world. An archaic system that had become rooted in the landscape, it was practically unmodernisable.

Its place in the hearts and social structures of the Mendip people had also become deeply embedded, but this was precariously dependent on the line's declining function as a major through route from the North to the South. And the Somerset coalfield had by then contracted into a small core of pits whose future was uncertain. The seams were difficult to work and labour was becoming harder to recruit. The writing had been on the wall for the S&D for many years.

The closure of the line in 1966 was a traumatic

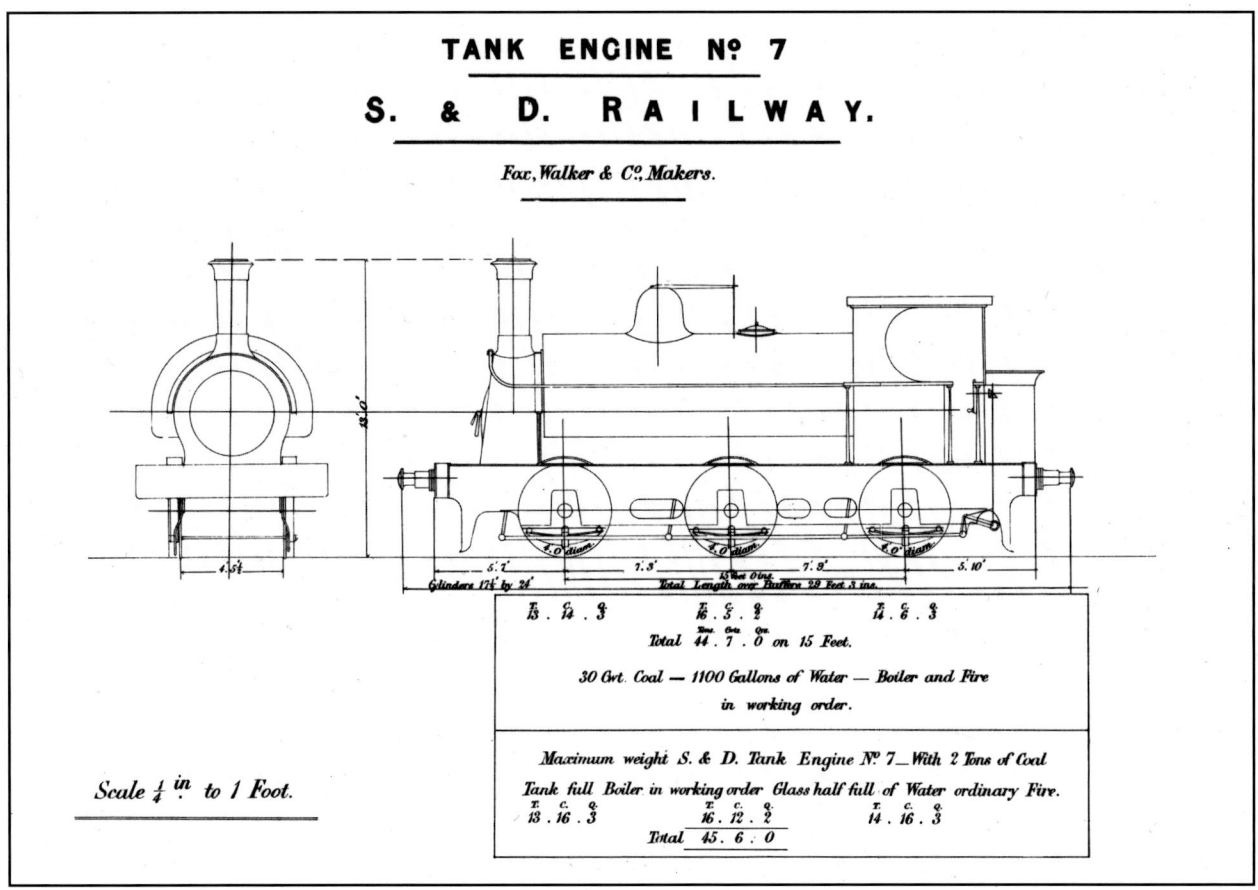

A small fleet of new locomotives was ordered to operate the Bath Extension. Six of these were 0-6-0 saddle tanks built in 1874 by Fox, Walker & Co of Bristol. This drawing was made for Captain Tyler's 1877 Board of Trade report and shows No 7, one of a second batch of such locomotives built in 1876. Tyler inspected the whole line, examining the state of the S&D's permanent way and the weight of traffic it had to support. He recommended complete renewal and relaying of the track, just two and a half years after opening.

experience for many people, but it failed to extinguish the spirit of the S&D. Many of the magnificent structures of the Bath Extension that Gale saw newly built have survived, though mostly rebuilt since his time, and while memories of the line are continually rekindled, its spirit lives on.

To illustrate this celebration of the Bath Extension I have used contemporary and later documents to counterpoint the narrative. Very few photographs exist from the line's earliest days, so I have included several views taken when much of the railway was being widened to accommodate double track in the 1880s and 90s. The extent of this civil engineering process, spread over some ten years, shows how under-resourced the original construction had been.

As a contrast to the optimism of this era I have interwoven a set of photographs which chronicle the decaying but wonderfully atmospheric final years of the line, when the last, wheezing steam trains ran and the forces of nature began to reclaim the stations, bridges, tunnels and viaducts.

I would like to thank Peter McGhie and the Somerset & Dorset Railway Trust for their assistance, particularly for allowing me to reproduce material from their collections. Many thanks also to Peter Cattermole for use of photographs from the S&DRT Maidment Collection on p.39 (top and bottom) and p.47; Dick Graham for the photograph on p.33 (top); Percy Lambert for the photograph on pp.36/7; Somerset Record Office for reproduction of the map on p.31 (top); and Bath Library for the photograph on p.6 (top). I hope that anyone who has been left uncredited will forgive my omissions.

Duncan Harper
OAKHILL
August 1998

Two views of the glass and iron structure which enclosed the passenger station at Bath. Above is a very early one which includes the plants and rock-work hiding the buffers in the foreground. Below is the penultimate service waiting to leave the station, the 4.25 to Templecombe, hauled by a suitably decorated Standard 2-6-4T No 80043. The date is 5th March 1966.

The
Somerset & Dorset Railway

Opening of the Bath Extension
1874

THE BATH TERMINUS

The situation of Bath is extremely beautiful. It has been termed the city of the Seven Hills from its being surrounded by Lansdown, Little Solsbury, Bannerdown, Kingsdown, Farleigh Down, Hampton Down, and Combe Down. The road to Bristol is a level one, and the same is the case with that to London, but if the excursionist goes in any other direction he must ascend a hill. With such a plenitude of Hills and Vales it will be readily imagined how pleasant is its situation, and how numerous are the beautiful walks and drives around the city. It is an absolute fact that one cannot leave Bath without being struck with the romantic beauty and picturesqueness of every space of ground. It is a place where every portion of the landscape is teeming with attractiveness amounting to fascination.

"What a handsome station", is the exclamation of visitors alighting on either of the spacious platforms of the terminus at Bath, and even residents are never tired of admiring it. The building was erected [in 1869] for the accommodation of the Midland passenger traffic, the goods department being on the other side of the river, but as the Somerset and Dorset Railway joined the Midland system about a quarter of a mile from the terminus and, as to erect another building would be inconvenient on account of the difficulty of obtaining space, it was mutually decided between the two companies to use it for both train services. In front of the station, which is of handsome design, fluted pillars with carved capitals support a neat balustrade. There is plenty of room in front of the station which is close to the fashionable neighbourhood of Green-park.

On entering the station the visitor is struck by its extreme lightness, good ventilation, and beauty of design. The plants and rock-work which hide the buffers, are a pleasing novelty. The numerous sidings within the station are spanned by a broad iron girder roof, covered with plate glass nearly a quarter of an inch in thickness. On either side there are spacious platforms covered to the extent of 100 yards, and uncovered they extend a similar distance. Charming views are obtained from these platforms into the fields which slope up the hills in the neighbourhood, the same being diversified by numerous elegant villas; the stores of the 2nd Somerset Militia are in the immediate foreground, and on the right the commencement of the rapidly growing village of Twerton.

To every train running over the Somerset and Dorset lines there will be attached through coaches. Messrs Spiers and Ponds have extremely convenient refreshment-rooms on the platform, which is also well supplied with waiting rooms, and in fact every other accommodation, whilst closely adjacent is the city of Bath, every portion of which is pregnant with interest.

THE NEW LINE ~ ITS HISTORY AND OBJECTS

Before railways became so common the Somerset coal field was considered to be well supplied with communication by canal and tramway accommodation, which afforded it superior communication with Bath and other places, whilst its central position made it satisfactorily situated with regard to the nearest towns of Dorset and those lying on the other side of the Mendips.

But when railways multiplied, and population, manufactures, and commerce of the country increased, and the demand for coal exhibited a corresponding growth, further development of the mineral resources of the district followed, and a general desire was manifested for better railway accommodation, other lines having advanced to within a few miles on every side.

Various projects to amend this condition of things were successively quashed, either from public apathy in reference to a scheme that it was universally admitted would be for the public good, or by rival desires of conflicting interests. Thus it is only a few years since that Radstock, the capital of the coal field, has enjoyed any railway communication at all, and this only for mineral traffic by way of Frome; scarcely a year since the North Somerset Railway, joining the district with Bristol, has been at work, whilst next week will see in operation another railway affording direct communication with Bath, and which, intersecting the county of Somerset from Bath on the north to Evercreech on the south, will more fully meet the wants and desires of the district.

It is also a curious coincidence that the mineral branch to Frome will concurrently be converted from broad to narrow gauge, in company with the whole of the south western branches of the Great Western Railway, and will hereafter, we believe, be opened for passenger traffic. The want of railway communication between Bath and Radstock has thus been long and severely felt. Local enterprise and wealth seemed unequal to the task, the vested interests that existed were considerable, and if not adequately compensated would of course oppose a scheme of any kind.

It seemed to be the natural task of the Great Western Company, whose interests so closely identified them with the district, to provide a railway between Bath and Radstock and the districts beyond; but the natural difficulties were immense, the Great Western Company were for many years not in a too flourishing state, and in addition to this they had the main portion of the traffic of the coal field and the surrounding district in their hands from the existence of their lines running to Bradford, Trowbridge, Westbury, Frome, Warminster, Shepton Mallet, and Wells, and from the fact that the Kennet and Avon canal is their property.

By and by, however, the Midland Company extended their system from Mangotsfield to Bath, thus affording this city and large sections of Somerset, Gloucester, and Wilts more convenient connexion with the north, but by an agreement with the Great Western the Company were prevented from going to Radstock. Then the desire for a railway from Bath to the coal field, and the towns on the other side of the Mendips showed itself with greater intensity, and ultimately a Bill was sent to Parliament in 1871, under the auspices of the Somerset and Dorset Railway Company, whose narrow gauge line of sixty-six miles, had proved of great local value, but had not been a commercial success on account of its being somewhat isolated from the traffic producing districts of this country, and other lines running from large towns.

The Bill of course evoked a great deal of opposition, the Great Western Railway Company and the North Somerset Railway Company (who had once obtained the power to construct a line from Bath to Radstock, but abandoned it), taking the lead, supported by several owners of property, whose land, it is worthy of remark, at this juncture will be considerably increased in value. The promoters of the Bill felt that the Bristol and Exeter broad gauge line was an inseparable obstacle in the way of through traffic from the Somerset and Dorset line by means of unbroken communication with Bristol, Gloucester, Birmingham, and the whole Midland and Northern systems of railway. The only narrow gauge communication was, they explained, by a circuitous route round by Salisbury. There was a considerable amount of traffic from Bournemouth, and large quantities of clay were sent from Poole to the Potteries, and large quantities of coal were sent from Radstock.

The Somerset and Dorset line had been completed, but its financial position was very unsatisfactory, resulting mainly from its want of narrow gauge communication with a through line, and it became evident that the proposed extension was the only means they had of improving their traffic and so getting out of their present difficulties. They expected to carry something like 70,000 tons of minerals a year, at an average charge of 1s 8d per ton all round, the passenger traffic being not more than 20,000 a-year. Of the anticipated increase, about one third would probably be through passengers, and the remainder local, at an average of 1s 6d per passenger.

This line has been constructed under the Authority of an Act of Parliament which received the Royal assent on the 21st August, 1871. This Act gave the Somerset and Dorset Railway Company power to raise by the issue of new shares, £360,000, and to borrow to the extent of £120,000 for the purpose of the extension railway. The line was not commenced at once, as doubtless the money market was not just then in the best state for "floating the undertaking," but in due course the contracts were taken by Messrs T. and C. Walker, of Westminster, who have been engaged in making this branch for about two years, and who have had sometimes as many as 3,000 hands employed on its works.

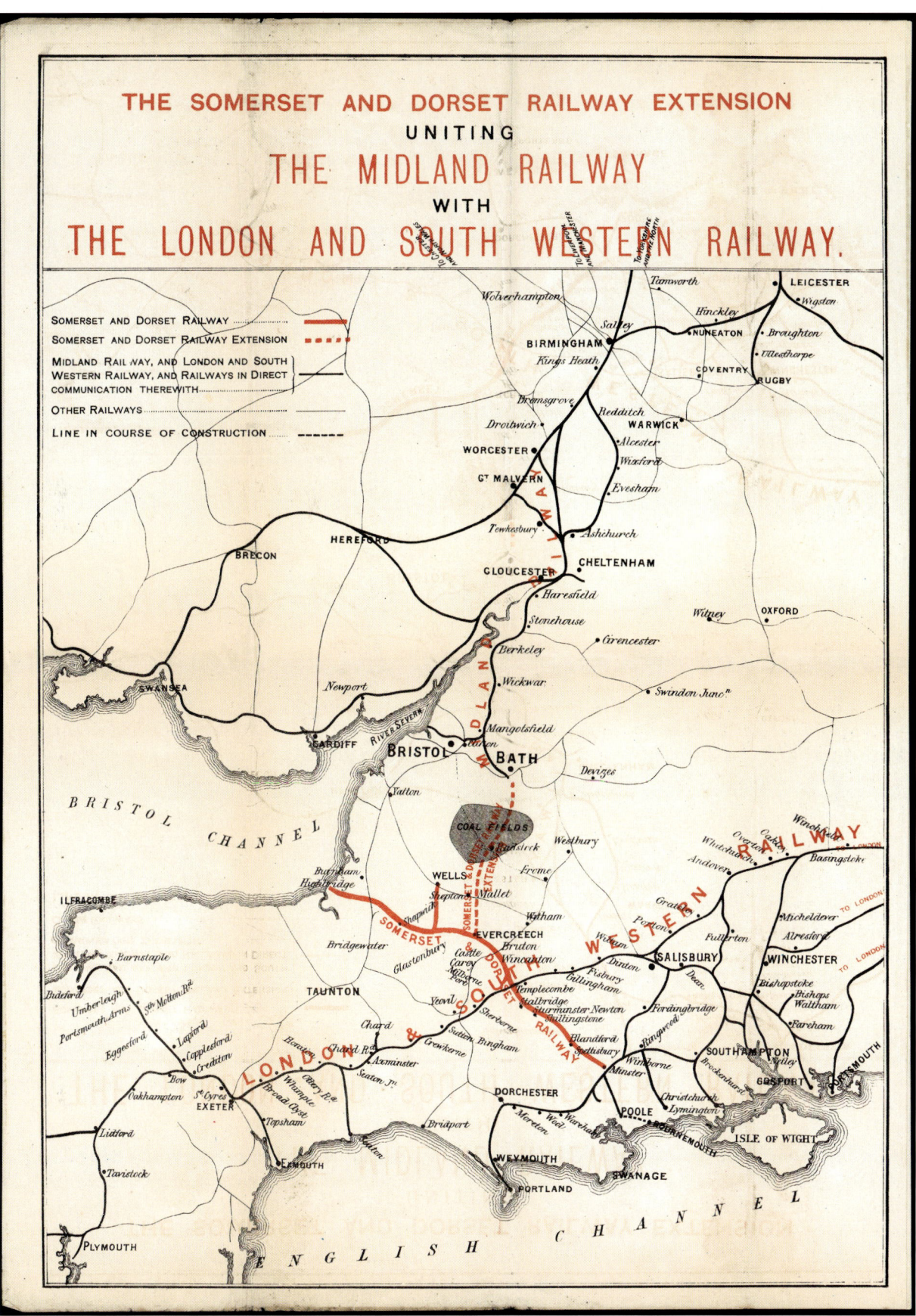

Somerset and Dorset Railway Company.

EXTENSION TO THE MIDLAND RAILWAY AT BATH.

(*Circular.*)

16, PARLIAMENT STREET, LONDON,
1st *January*, 1873.

I am requested by the Trustees to send you the annexed Warrant for the Interest on your Extension Shares in this Company to the 31st December, 1872.

I am, your obedient Servant,

To *Miss Mary Hostage*

ROBERT A. READ,
Managing Director.

Winnington Bank
Registered Proprietor. *Northwich*

EXTENSION £20 SHARES.

INTEREST STATEMENT TO THE 31ST DECEMBER, 1872.

	Six Months' Interest from 30th June, 1872, to 31st December, 1872, at 5 per cent.
On 25 Shares at £20 Per Share £ 50	£ 12 10 0

Half-yearly interest on the Bath Extension shares was paid promptly in 1873. But the company faced bankruptcy and the railway was only completed after the contractor agreed to accept shares and Lloyds Bonds as payment for the construction work. The map on the previous page and the progress report opposite are from the prospectus for the final share issue.

The local and general advantages will be many and various; they will not only be distributed along the line, but will affect the Midland company at this end, and the Somerset and Dorset and the South Western railways, which exist at the other end of the line, and the districts with which they communicate.

First and foremost stands the city of Bath and its neighbourhood, the inhabitants of which will largely participate in the advantages arising from the construction of the line. It is true that Bath people burn a great deal of north country and Forest of Dean coal, but they mainly depend for their supply of "black diamonds" on the pits in the Somerset field. The coal is durable in quality, and, therefore, the most economical that local consumers are aquainted with. But the colliery proprietors have been excluded from fair competition in the Bath market, on account of the absence of such railway facilities as other coal producing districts enjoyed. All excuses for high prices will now be swept away. Cheaper coal will be a great benefit to all classes in Bath at the present time.

It is well known among the tradesmen of this city, whose merchandise was patronised by the inhabitants of the coal field that since the North Somerset line to Bristol has been opened, the colliers and their families have forsaken the Bath road, with its uncertain and uncomfortable conveyances, and carried their money to Bristol. Ask any of the traders likely to be affected by such a diminution in customers, and they will tell you that the falling off has been serious. To Bristol, the increase of business has been correspondingly great. It is therefore hoped, and there can be no doubt that the expected advantage of opening the line to Bath, which has by long association become the favourite market of the people of this district, will be realized, that the considerable amount of trade she so long enjoyed but has recently lost, will be regained, with an additional meed of custom of no inconsiderable magnitude.

SOMERSET AND DORSET RAILWAY COMPANY.

Extension to the Midland Railway at Bath.

ENGINEER'S REPORT.

Engineer's Office,
January 1st, 1873.

Gentlemen,

The works of the Extension to the Midland Railway at Bath, have, since my last report, continued to be actively and vigorously carried forward throughout nearly the entire length of the line, and great progress has been made on all the heaviest parts of the work.

Contracts have been concluded for the greater part of the land, and more than one half has been paid for and is in possession of the Contractors and fenced off.

The following is a summary of the state of the works up to the present time:—

On the first section of 10 miles upwards of 135,000 yards of earthwork have been executed, and in the heavy cuttings near Shepton Mallet headings are being driven, as the face of the cuttings proceeds, to facilitate the excavation and removal of the earth.

A large bridge near Evercreech, of four 30-feet side arches and girders, is completed, all but the superstructure.

A viaduct at Prestleigh, of eleven arches of 30-feet span, is completed all but the superstructure.

A large and lofty viaduct at Shepton Mallet is well advanced, both abutments and five piers being completed, and the materials for the arches are on the ground.

Of the remaining works, twelve bridges are completed, except the parapets and copings, or are ready to receive the girders, and considerable progress has been made with four others.

On the second section of 10 miles, where the works are comparatively light, the cuttings and embankments are in active operation, more than 50,000 yards of earthwork having been executed. The public road bridge, at Chilcompton, and the foundations of the Chilcompton viaduct are completed; a public road bridge near Chilcompton is nearly up to girder level; considerable progress has been made in the masonry of the long bridge, at the south end of the deep cutting at Chilcompton; a bridge crossing the road near the site of the Midsomer Norton Station is more than half completed, and two bridges between Radstock and Midford are in a very forward state.

Upon the remaining section the works generally are well advanced, and upwards of 180,000 yards of earthwork are executed,

The tunnel under Combe Down, near Bath, 1,826 yards in length, is excavated for a distance of 1,180 yards, and the north face of masonry is completed. The tunnel under the Devonshire Buildings, a length of 440 yards, is well advanced, a heading will be completed throughout by the middle of next month, and the masonry lining from the north end is completed through a length of 52 yards.

The Midford viaduct of eight 30 feet arches of great height and four 3 arch bridges are completed with the exception of the superstructure, and one other bridge is up to girder bed.

The Contractors have a full supply of excellent plant upon the ground, including four locomotive engines, three traction engines, ten portable engines, and sixty horses, and I am happy to be able to state that the quality of the work is of the most satisfactory character, and the rate of progress such as to leave no reason to doubt their ability to complete the line by the time stipulated in the contract, namely, the 31st of December next.

I am,

Gentlemen,

Your obedient Servant,

F. G. SLESSOR,
Resident Engineer.

To

*The Chairman and Directors
of the Somerset and Dorset Railway Company.*

The substitution of a short and comfortable journey of half-an-hour between Radstock and Bath, for a couple of hours crawling over formidable hills, cannot fail to attract a greater number of visitors to this city on ordinary as well as on special occasions. In confirmation of this prediction we need only state how popular Bath has become with the inhabitants of the villages lying this side of Bristol since the extension of the Midland Railway. To the many scores who have business relations in this neighbourhood, or those places to the south, the railway will be looked upon as a positive blessing. Apart from the quantity of coal that will be sent over the line, the existence of so extensive a seat of industry in the centre of the line cannot fail to be of great value to everybody concerned therewith, and to still further develop the producing capabilities of the district.

The viands and beverages of which we diurnally partake must show that there is a close alliance between the wants and interests of town and country. Those who manufacture cheese and butter and raise vegetables, will find their time economised and their products enhanced in value by the existence of a more expeditious means of transit, and thus all along the line, whether we look at collieries, farms, gardens, or breweries we shall find that the great majority will hail the opening of the line as an individual and collective benefit, which will contribute to the general happiness, prosperity, and convenience.

During the present summer a branch of railway, from Poole to Bournemouth, has been opened, which will enable a passenger to travel from Birmingham to Poole or Bournemouth without changing; and as Poole is one of the nearest ports to Cherbourg, an active train service may divert into this route the stream of traffic which must exist between the north and France.

The benefits that are expected to be realized by travellers from this city [Bath] **are, without doubt, its giving a more direct route to Bournemouth – the "Hampshire Torquay" – and affording the much needed access to competing lines for passengers travelling to Exeter and Barnstaple on the one hand, or Southampton and Portsmouth on the other. Possibly this fact has operated very considerably in inducing the Great Western Railway Company to give greater facilities for travelling over their branch lines to Salisbury and Weymouth. We trust the directors of the Somerset and Dorset Railway will make such arrangements, and frame such regulations with respect to the new railway to Evercreech, as will speedily redeem the present character of the parent line, the initials of which – S. and D.R. – have facetiously been interpreted as "Slow and Dirty Railway."**

The new line was inspected by Colonel Rich, on behalf of the Board of Trade on the 25th, 26th, and 27th of June, when it is understood that gentleman, having carefully tested and examined the various bridges, and other heavy works, passed the same. Since then the stations have been inspected, and passed; but various modifications of the works and sundry details were required to be attended to before the certificate of the Board of Trade could be isssued. The needful works having been carried out, the inspector, on Friday last [17th July], **went down the whole line, which occupied him all day. On his return, he having intimated his satisfaction with the arrangements, the Company lost no time in issuing notices of their intention to open on Monday last** [20th July].

On Saturday [18th July] *several trial trains ran over the line in order to test the speed and to familiarize the men with the road and observe the working of the telegraph apparatus. Amongst the passengers were Messrs Read (managing director), A. Difford (secretary)* [Abraham Difford was also the Traffic Superintendent], *Walker (contractor), Wood (general inspector), Fisher (locomotive superintendent)* [B.S.Fisher had transferred from the Taff Vale Railway that year], *Saunders (telegraphic contractor)* [The Block Telegraph had been installed by J.B.Saunders of Cardiff], *Lean and Priestly (contractors' engineers).*

The first run was to Temple Combe and back, and, so far as the new line was concerned, capital time was kept, and the trains ran with remarkable smoothness considering the line was freshly constructed.

The whole of the works have been carried out under the direction of Mr A.Priestly as contractors' chief engineer; and extend from the junction with the Midland Railway at Bath to the junction with the main line of the Somerset and Dorset Railway Company, near Evercreech, a distance of 25¾ miles.

THE LINE ~ ITS ROUTE AND GEOLOGICAL AND ANTIQUARIAN FEATURES

Under this head we propose to give the districts, towns, and villages through which the line passes, together with any item of interest connected with them, the strata met with, and in fact a detailed account of the railway itself.

Moger's bridge (No 13), a brick and stone arch springing across the cutting in Lyncombe Vale. This photograph, taken shortly after closure, clearly demonstrates the curvature and 1:50 gradient of the single track that S&D trains were required to tackle.

It has been stated that Mr Brunel, in his later years, considered railways with many curves were safer for travelling than those which were straight. If so, the new line may be considered as one of the safest in the kingdom, as it is by no means straight; in fact, it is almost a succession of curves, resembing somewhat the South Devon line, which resemblance is also strengthened by the steep gradients, one in fifty being frequent. The line, speaking generally, ascends from Bath to the Mendips, which it crosses at about the height of Lansdown, and then descends to the junction.

GRADIENTS

From the S&DR Book of Rules and Regulations

The ruling gradient of the Line is 1 in 50.

Enginemen and Guards in ascending the gradients must keep a good look-out along their train, and have their brakes ready to apply instantly, should any of the Vehicles break away.

All Goods Trains must be stopped in the deep cutting near Masbury, (at about 18 miles from Bath,) and also at Canard's Grave, (just South of Shepton Mallet,) and before commencing the descent, the Guards must pin down the brakes of every third Wagon.

In descending the gradients no attempt must be made to make up lost time, and the speed of the train must be carefully regulated by the Brakes of the engine, and (in the case of passenger trains) if necessary by the application of the continuous brake.

The speed of Heavy Goods or Mineral trains in descending the 1 in 50 gradients must not exceed ten miles an hour.

As many of the stations, including the Junction with the Midland Railway at Bath, are approached on the 1 in 50 gradient, strict attention must be paid to these instructions.

Should a train in any case be unable to proceed up any of the Inclines, it must be divided, and the first portion of the train must proceed to the next station ahead, where it must be left, and the engine will then return for the second portion.

The Guard accompanying the first portion of the Train must, on arriving at the Station ahead, show a Red Flag, and instantly communicate to the Station Agent the fact of the train having divided so as to prevent the possibility of his starting any other Train, or signalling "Line Clear" for a following Train, until the second portion has been brought in.

SHUNTING OF TRAINS

The utmost care and vigilance must be used to prevent trucks from running past the points and escaping down the inclines while shunting is going on, during which all signals must be kept at danger.

The stations are all of the same pattern, but differ in size in accordance with the requirements of the place. They are substantially composed of blue lias stone with Bath or Doulting stone dressings, and slate tile roofs. From the front wall of each there stands a wooden verandah, the edges of which are hung with Vandyked vallance [i.e. the decorative edging composed of notches and points]. In nearly all the stations there are two waiting rooms and a booking office. The buildings are of English architecture, and present an attractive appearance, though they are all but one storey high. The platform of each station is covered with gravel, there being at the edge two courses of blue bricks, the outer of which is rounded off.

As the line is a single one, there is no positive necessity for crossing the rails, but as there are generally two lines at the stations, it would be desirable at some time to carry over at least the platforms of the more important stations, and to start the trains from opposite sides. This would of course necessitate bridges, or should do so. No provision, however, appears to have been made for doubling the line throughout, so that it may be presumed the traffic is not expected to be enormous. [The intermediate stations provided at this time with loops and concomitant signal and telegraph apparatus appear to have been Wellow, Radstock, Midsomer Norton, Binegar, Shepton Mallet and Evercreech Village.]

The home and distant signals in connexion with each station are worked from the station itself, the signal levers being above ground, and the machinery in a covered pit. **The signalling is effected by Saxby and Farmer's patent levers with locking apparatus attached. The rods of the levers are painted different colours, and are numbered on brass plates to distinguish them. The pointsmen are also assisted by large brass plates fixed behind the row of levers, explanatory of their names and operation; and also by a plan of the line at that particular station, showing where the points and signals are, and the mode of operation. The levers are in covered boxes on the platform, and therefore, like the pointsman, are easy of access.**

The point is set with a lever, and by pulling another a bolt is run into a slot, and the point tightly held in its place. Unless the points are closed the bolt cannot be run home, and the switchman is made aware of danger. The same lever that runs the bolt into the slot also turns the signal to "line clear," and a train cannot come up till the point is properly set. The imperfect action of points has always been a fruitful source of accidents, so that intending travellers on the line will look upon the introduction of these points with satisfaction. **Close to each box is a clock, with chocolate coloured face and white figures. Unfortunately all the clocks were more or less behind hand on Monday last.** [A cast-iron faced clock survived at Midford for many years, made by Dell & Co. of Bristol in 1874. The mechanism operated an interior and a platform face.]

SIGNALS
From the S&DR Book of Rules and Regulations

Semaphore signals have been erected throughout this line, and in addition to the Distant and Home Signals, Starting Signals are placed at all stations where there are Loops for up and down trains.

Trains not timed to stop at a station must have all these signals kept against them until "Line Clear" and "Train on Line" have been obtained from the Station ahead.

When two trains are timed to cross, one of which is not timed to stop at the crossing station, the train which is timed to stop must be first admitted to the station and brought to a stand before the signals are lowered for a non-stopping train.

The bleak aspect of the second highest station on the S&D at Binegar, over 750 ft up on the windswept Mendips, photographed shortly after closure. The architecture has a unity of style and is typical of the Bath Extension stations, though the original building has been enlarged and complemented by the later signalbox and waiting shelter.

It must be understood that the lowering of the distant and home signals only indicate that the line is clear up to the station, and the station must not be passed until the starting signal at the further end of the loop has also been lowered.

In all cases where there are two arms facing in the same direction, the upper arm is for the left-hand road and the lower arm for the right-hand road.

In all cases where the Distant Signals are not visible from the Station Platform, Electric Repeaters have been provided. Particular attention must be given to these, and any defect in working must be immediately reported to the Engineer, and the usual report made to the Traffic Superintendent.

All the Signals interlock with the Points, and there are Catch Points placed inside all switches leading from sidings on to the Main Line or Loops.

At each station there is a siding for the purpose, we suppose, of allowing trains to pass each other. The whole of the rails throughout the line are of first rate quality, and of strong durable pattern. At this end of the line the "packing" between the rails (which are all laid upon transoms placed across, and not longitudinally, as is the practice upon the main line of the Great Western Railway,) is of gravel. Near Radstock the cinders from the colliery engines are used for this purpose, and at other points broken stone, which being of white lias, presents a clean appearance. The whole of the work on the line has been heavy, and especially so at this end. The viaducts are numerous and are all very substantially built of white or blue lias, roughly faced, with brick turned arches. They are all very similar in design, and are handsome structures, the piers supporting the arches being graceful but strong. As the branch is only a single line the viaducts are narrower than we have been accustomed to see on broad gauge double lines in this locality. There are numerous occupation bridges for the accommodation of the occupiers on either side of the line, and bridges for road traffic. Some of these have been built of bricks, many thousands of which were moulded from clay dug out of the cuttings, and others of lias stone obtained in the same way. There are goods sheds adjacent to the stations where it is thought the traffic will be sufficient to render them necessary.

BATH *to* RADSTOCK

The first train left Bath at 7.25 on Monday morning [20th July]. Very few passengers went by it. Probably comparatively few were able to avail themselves of it at so short a notice. A considerable number of spectators, however, watched the train as it left the departure platform of the Midland terminus, which arrangement caused some little confusion, as passengers for Bristol and the North had, in consequence, to start from the arrival side.

There was a little amiable diplomacy at the booking office to obtain the first ticket and judging from his appearance the individual who secured the honour was well pleased. With praiseworthy punctuality the train, having waited for the arrival of the first train from the north, steamed quietly out of the station, no articulate demonstration being made. About thirty passengers booked to different stations on the line, the greatest distance booked being to Evercreech, although the next contained several passengers for more distant places. The first train left at 7.25 am, and kept good time during its run on the new line. Mr Difford, the secretary of the Somerset and Dorset Company, was amongst the passengers in the first train, whilst on the engine drawing it was Mr Fisher, the locomotive superintendent.

BATH JUNCTION

From the S & D R Book of Rules and Regulations

The Junction with the Midland Railway is at a point half a mile from the Bath Station.

In approaching and leaving the Midland Railway, the trains of this Company will be controlled by the signals and other regulations of the Midland Railway Company, and the servants of this Company must receive and act upon the instructions of the Officials of that Company while upon that Line.

The junction is exactly opposite the Twerton Hayes, and the points face Bath. Leaving the junction the line runs along an embankment in a south-westerly direction across the Twerton road, close to the turnpike, where there is an iron girder bridge, supported by massive circular columns, and a viaduct of several brick arches which carries the line up to a high embankment running through the field between the Twerton road and the Great Western line. **The Great Western Railway is crossed close to its first occupation bridge from Twerton, by a brick bridge, which, in accordance with the provisions of the Act, consists of "a centre opening sufficient for two lines of rails, and two side openings, sufficient for one additional line of rails."**

Beyond is a slight cutting through marl. Up to this point the course of the line has the shape of a half circle, which it was necessary for the line to describe before commencing its course towards the Wells-road, an embankment of considerable depth carries us into a cutting of stiff clay of a wet nature and bluish hue above which was found a bed of gravel containing many fossils and mammoth tusks. Whilst passing up to this cutting we have had time to notice that the line commands a most interesting view which embraces the village of Twerton, the Park, the High-common, Lansdown, Beacon-hill, Hampton-down, Beechen-cliff, in the midst of which lies the city, compact and clean. The upper end of the cutting is occupied by a lengthy platform and an attendants' house, both of which stand on the southern side of the line. Here the tickets of up trains are collected or inspected.

BATH TICKET PLATFORM

From the S & D R Book of Rules and Regulations

This Platform is placed about half a mile from the Junction with the Midland Railway, and all Up Trains must stop there as shown in the Working Time Book.

The Starting Signal must be kept at danger, and no Up Train is to pass this Platform until "Line Clear" has been received from the Bath Junction Signalman according to the code of the Midland Regulations, and the Starting Signal Arm has been lowered accordingly.

Next follows a long and deep embankment across the Oldfield-valley, there again a charming view is obtained. To the left we get a full view of Lansdown and Kelston Round Hill, and beneath the village of

The romantic Lyncombe Vale. The southbound 1.15pm from Bath charges up through the secluded valley, crossing the three-arch Watery Bottom viaduct on a wintry day, 6th March 1965. Despite several of the bridges being rebuilt, the tunnels would have been too expensive to widen and this section of railway from Bath Junction to Midford remained a single track until it closed.

Weston, snugly embosomed, is a combe formed by the two eminences. At the end of this embankment we enter another deep marl cutting, which increases in depth until we enter Bloomfield tunnel, which is about a quarter of a mile in length, and straight with the exception of a curve at the end opposite to that we enter. The water bearing strata was here tapped, and a large quantity runs out of the tunnel. If the company had to pay compensation for depriving the numerous wells in the neighbourhood of their springs, they may by and by find a favourable opportunity of disposing of it, as Twerton is a growing district, and a reservoir constructed in the fields near the tunnel would admirably supply the whole village. The tunnel throughout is strongly lined with masonry; blue lias stone being used.

On emerging from the tunnel we find ourselves crossing the romantic Lyncombe-vale, on one side of which are green fields, and on the other neatly cultivated and fruitful market gardens. Immediately after we are in a rugged oolite cutting, which runs through the fields of Mr. Moger, for whose convenience a fly arch bridge, over which the footpath to Fox-hill passes, has been erected. Lyncombe House, Mr. Moger's residence, stands at the bottom of a valley which runs up the hill towards Warner's Cottage, where it gradually slopes out and disappears in the hillside. The view from the front of the house up this glen, fringed as it was with trees, was pretty in the extreme, and although it has been damaged by the passage of the line, yet the planting of the embankments with shrubs and ivy and the substitution of a handsome viaduct of light design has lessened what in a picturesque sense might have been looked upon as an evil. **This arch, by the aid of turf, plants, and other garden accessories, has been made as pleasing an object from the house as a railway bridge, perhaps, could possibly be under the circumstances.**

Directly we have crossed the viaduct we shoot into the north end of the Combe Down tunnel, and the transition from the pleasing rural scenery to the cool gloom of the tunnel is a novelty. Combe Down tunnel is a mile and a quarter in length. At either end there

This signal diagram blueprint of 1933 shows the original single line from Bath passing through Midford station and splitting out into double track on the massive eight-arch viaduct (Gale mistakenly counted ten). When the viaduct was widened in 1892, the signal box was built and the junction of the old single- and new double-track sections was made at the Bath end of the viaduct. The junction was shifted to the south end on 9th April 1933 to allow trains to pass over it at higher speeds. This alteration is visible on the original blueprint.

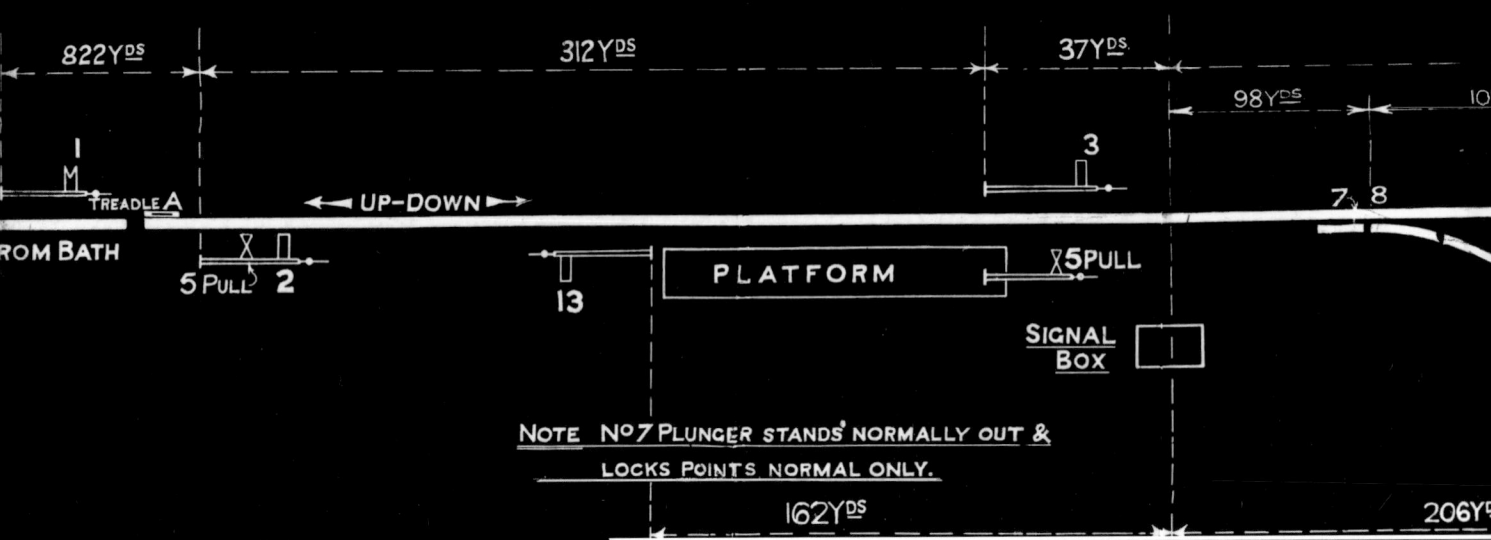

is a curve of a few score yards, and the remainder of the distance it is straight. About 200 yards at either end were the only places where it was found necessary to introduce continuous masonry, but in other parts where the ceiling was faulty lining has been resorted to. It is cut through a kind of sandy rock, very tough and secure. It occupied about eighteen months to make the tunnel, which, like several other modern borings is only large enough for a single line of rails. The ventilation is very good, and although we rode on an engine and had the benefit of the smoke and steam, we experienced no inconvenience. The tunnel was constructed without the aid of a shaft. The water bearing stratum is Fuller's earth and, being above the tunnel, keeps it dry throughout the greater portion, and the springs of Combe Down remain uninjured. The existence of bands of ironstone at short intervals give the tunnel great natural strength. There are large man-holes at intervals of fifty feet, these refuges being equally distributed on either side. The excellence of the supervision may be inferred from the fact that when the gangs of men who commenced the work on either end met in the centre of the tunnel they were only a few inches out of the straight line. The southern mouth of the tunnel is on the steep escarpment that lies just behind Combe Down. The portion of the tunnel which is farthest below the surface of the earth is about 200 yards from the southern entrance, where the rails are upwards of 350 feet below the surface.

The scenery on again coming into daylight is delightful, and after a brief glance at the romantic woods that lie in the direction of Midford Castle, we run across the handsome viaduct that stands in the valley, on either side of which are the ponds below Tucking Mills. This viaduct is composed of six arches, which are from 50 to 70 feet high. Between the mouth of the tunnel and the viaduct there is space for a station, if required. The scenery up to this point has been of a rapidly changing character, but now we have the broad open valley of Midford before us, the richly wooded grounds attached to the park on the right, the cultivated meadows, through which the trout stream and the canal runs in the bottom, and then the arable and pasture land occasionally relieved by woods and timber stretching away to the crest of the hill on the other side. As we enter Midford-park there is a cutting in the inferior oolite and as we leave it a similar piece of work occurs.

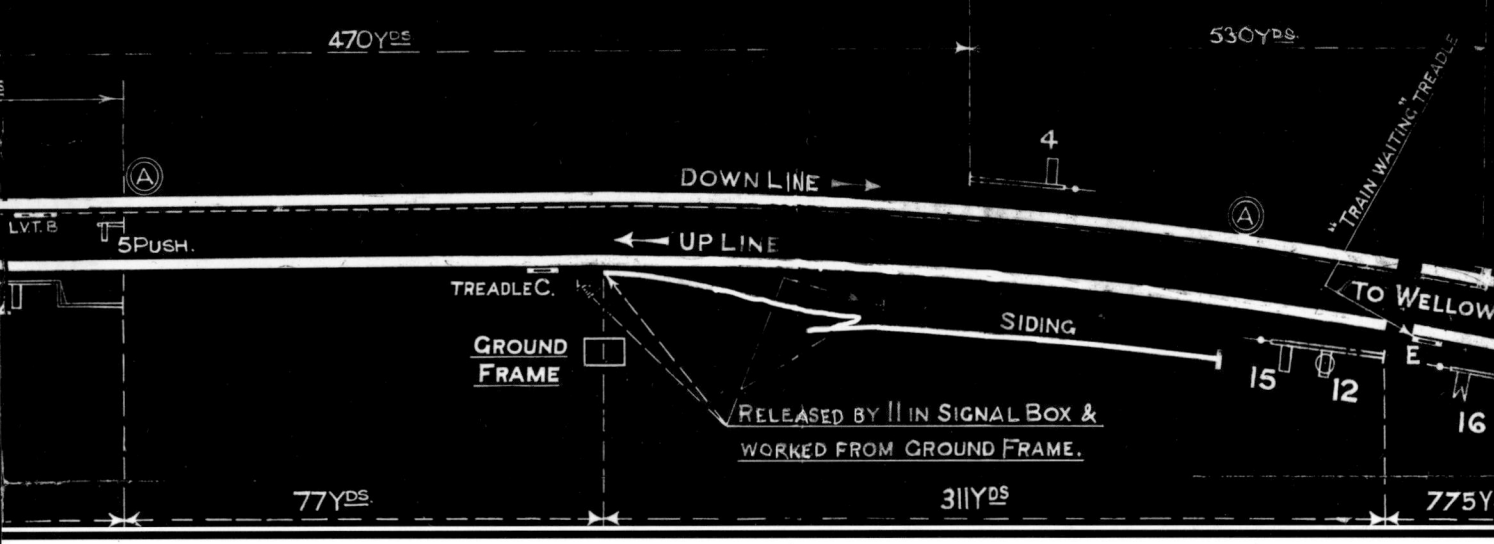

Midford station and the little village of Midford, which stands in two counties and five or seven parishes is just afterwards reached. The platform is beneath a wall of rock, and the station, which is the only exception to the rule laid down above, is built of wood. The line is reached from the high road by an inclined path. This station accommodates the folks of Combe Down, which is a mile away, and Combehay, Monkton Combe, Southstoke, Englishcombe and Limpley Stoke. Freshford, and Charterhouse Hinton, with its interesting Abbey are within easy distances as well as Conkwell and Monkton Farleigh on the other side of the river. Norton St Philip will perhaps be one of the largest contributors to this station, as it is only a mile or two up the hill on the Frome road.

On leaving Midford station we at once cross the Midford viaduct, an extensive piece of work, there being ten large arches, the highest of which is 55 feet. **It is erected over the Midford valley, and crosses the turnpike-road to Frome, the Somersetshire Coal Canal, and the brook. The viaduct commands a very beautiful view of the Midford valley. By the side of this structure, a new road with the bridge over the canal has been made in accordance with an agreement with the late Mr Gore Langton, for the convenience of persons coming from Midford and the neighbourhood. The railway between Midford and Radstock follows to a very considerable extent the route of the tram-road formerly belonging to the Company of Proprietors of the Somersetshire Coal Canal Navigation. This old "railway" was constructed by that company some seventy years since, in lieu of a canal in the Wellow valley, and was made on its towing path.** Sections of the trench may still be seen, but the course of the line has cut across the route of both the intended canal and the tramway. **The tram road, with all its branches and works, was sold by its proprietors to the Railway Company under their Act.**

The route takes us over several short embankments, through several equally short cuttings in the oolite, over a viaduct of four arches of 30 feet span each, and then the train draws up at Wellow, about 6 miles from Bath. *On nearing Wellow there was a greater number of people about than was seen at any other point, and the approach of the train was heralded by a merry peal.* **Here the bells of the fine old church rang out merrily, it is**

Somerset & Dorset Railway
EXTENSION TO BATH
And
E. L. R. B. Gale.

Land required colored Red

REFERENCE   A. R. P.

No. 173.   0 . 1 . 7.

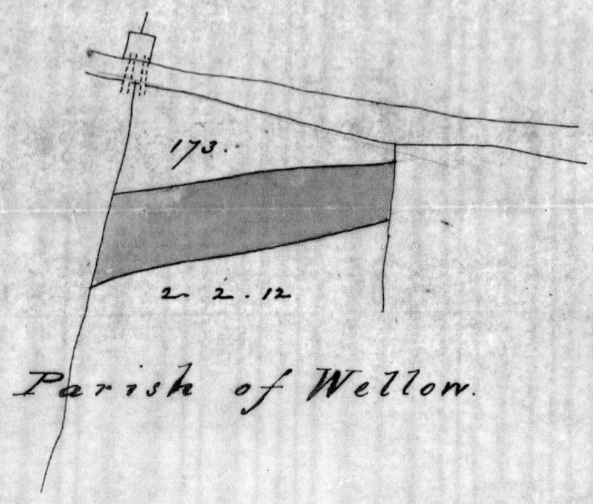

173

2 . 2 . 12

Parish of Wellow.

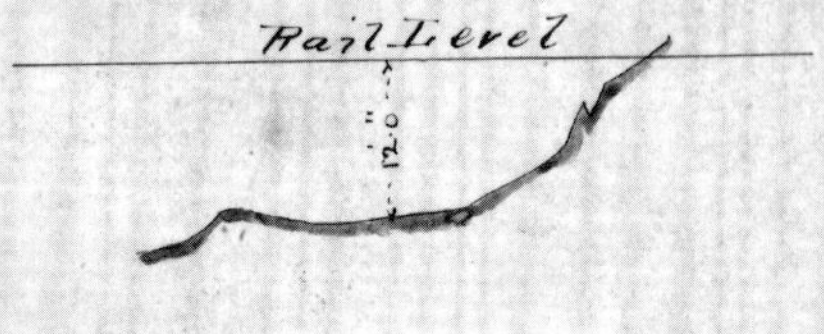

Rail Level

Scales. HORIZONTAL 2 CHAINS TO AN INCH
VERTICAL 20 FEET TO AN INCH

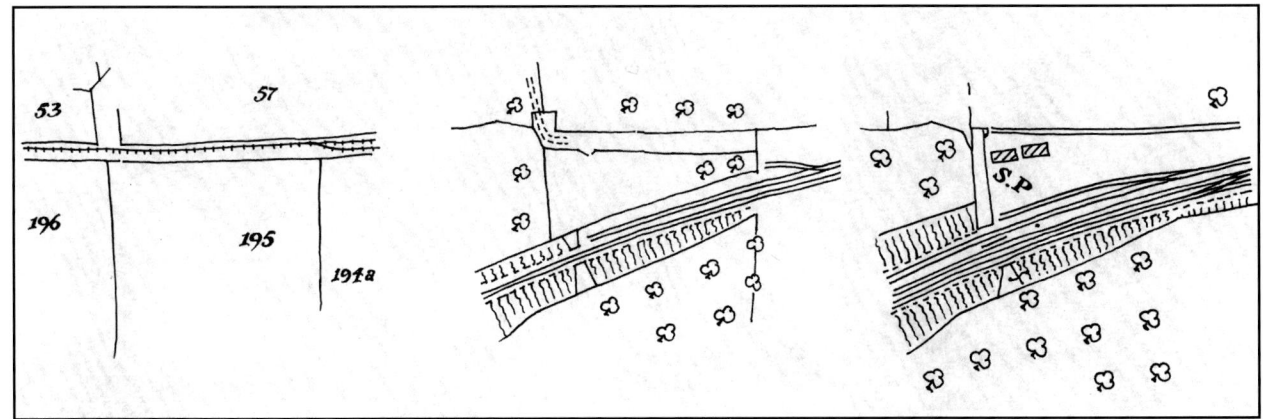

The plan opposite shows a plot of land at Wellow which the S&D intended to purchase from E.L.Gale in 1872. Shown just above the strip, which is coloured in red, the line of the old Somersetshire Coal Canal tramway is delineated. This had been laid along the towpath of the canal in 1815 between Midford and Radstock, and was bought by the S&D for £20,000. The drawings above show how this small plot was altered over the years, from the tramway (1839 Tithe map) to the single-track S&D Bath Extension crossing a farm track by a stone arch (1886 OS map) to the doubled S&D main line, widened in 1894 and with a long goods siding carried on an iron bridge beside the arch (1931 OS map). The bridge (No24) was known as Store's Bridge.

presumed in honour of the opening of the new line, which will certainly be a convenience to the owners of the well stocked rosaries and strawberry gardens, for which Wellow is noted.

The village is very prettily situated, and a few hours can be here spent with profitable enjoyment. Above the village and to the south lies the ancient Briton ridgeway, which runs along the highest table land in Somerset, and commands a view that outrivals anything of the kind in the neighbourhood. Combe Down, Lansdown, and intermediate places are plainly seen, while cultivated upland and vales diversified by pretty villages, are agreeably mixed. The station here will accommodate Dunkerton, where the old Roman Fosse Way may be seen, Camerton, where there are pits producing coal celebrated for its gas-making qualities, Faulkland, Whiteoxmead, whose name smacks of British origin, Single-hill, a populous hamlet, and other out-lying places.

All along the route great interest was manifested in the opening of the line, but there was scarcely any merrymaking. The people of the village of Wellow enjoyed themselves in a quiet way on the occasion. As each train ran past, the bells were rung and as more than a dozen trains ran into and out of Wellow station the merry peals prevailed throughout the day. The neat little station had been decorated by Mr Wilmot, the station-master, assisted by some of the villagers, Mr Jeakway, the veteran rose grower, contributing several pretty baskets containing nicely arranged bouquets. One enthusiastic resident had lavishly decorated himself.

His head, which a countryman irreverently termed a "top-not," was bedecked with numerous large hollyhocks and other flowers, and as he strolled about alone in his glory, he protested again and again that he never expected to have lived to see a railway at Wellow.

In the evening nearly all the inhabitants of the village assembled at the station and one elderly man who was said to be quite an infant in regard to railway travelling was unmercifully chaffed about a little mishap that occurred to him in returning from his primal trip to Bath and back. In his inexperience he had imagined that somebody would ask him to leave the carriage and when the train moved on without this mark of deference being paid him he practically shouted "Stop the train, stop the train." This request was not complied with, and the traveller had to go to Radstock and return by the next train. On arriving at Wellow he calmly assured his friends that he had been to Radstock "on business."

Leaving Wellow station we continue along the broad vale which leads to Radstock. The gradient on leaving Wellow is very easy up towards Radstock. A short distance before reaching Wellow station there is a viaduct, and a few hundred yards beyond it there is another. Near the latter there is a cutting 36 feet deep cut through a blue greasy clay, the slipperyness of which gave the contractors some trouble. Single Hill is next reached. This hamlet is mainly inhabited by colliers, who have petitioned the company for a station. The prayer has not yet been acceded to, but is still under consideration of the Directors.

Soon after leaving Single Hill, adjacent to which is a place called Double Hill, we catch sight of the first evidence of the Somerset coal field in the shape of the smoke arising from Foxcote pit. A mile from Radstock is the Home-farm viaduct of seven arches being one for the road and six for the farming purposes.

In the bottom of the valley and close by the stream is the Writhlington pit, and a couple of hundred feet high on the opposite side of the hill is Braysdown colliery, which is connected with the line by a steep gradient down which the trucks are let by wire ropes. **Passing the small church at Writhlington, and the Upper and Lower Writhlington pits, under the bridge of the line from the Tyning works belonging to the Countess Waldegrave, who also owns the Ludlow pit on the other side, the train draws up at the Radstock station, eleven miles from Bath.**

Here a great portion of the interest of the line centres. For several years Radstock has been a growing district. It has long contained the elements necessary for an increase in its size, but the requirements, notably of house accommodation, have been absent. In addition to the great coal trade carried on at Radstock there are two busy manufactories of railway waggons, and the celebrated Midland Wagon Company whose chief workshops are at Birmingham, and who have repairing shops at all the principal stations, are about to establish a depot here for that purpose, and will erect a building. Both the branches of railway which now pass Radstock have been constructed on the narrow gauge principle, which, as it is exclusively used on the Midland and South Western lines and as the Great Western is adopting, the plan must be considered as one of universal use. It cannot but be concluded that this rapid growth of railway accommodation whilst affording much convenience to the inhabitants will also have a highly beneficial effect upon commerce, which will be developed to a much greater extent than at present, for it must be remembered that both the road and canal communication – which have until recently been the sole arteries of trade – have been in winter greatly dependent upon the weather which has restricted the trade.

The village, though large, is not compactly built. The market-place is in the centre, and large quantities of all the necessaries of life are here sold on Saturdays. A street then runs a considerable distance along the Wells-road, where the houses have largely multiplied in recent years. Another street is in the direction of the Frome road, where are situate the extensive mechanical works and offices of the Countess Waldegrave's collieries. The workshops are in the shape of a quadrangle, and the offices, in front of which is a clock, overlook the block of buildings.

To the north of Radstock proper is The Tyning, a populous neighbourhood standing on an elevated plateau, affording a view of the whole place. It is in this neighbourhood and on the slopes of the eminence that Lady Waldegrave, who owns the manor, and whose husband Lord Carlingford, who recently spoke of the place as "the future borough of Radstock," has made provision for the erection of 300 cottages, and we also hear that facilities will be afforded for private building enterprise. Therefore there can be no doubt now of the rapid growth of Radstock. Slightly beyond the Tyning-pit stand a couple of long rows of cottages, which are inhabited by miners employed at the Radstock collieries, and to which are attached well kept gardens.

The parish church is an ancient edifice, dedicated to St Nicholas, but lies low and does not display itself. There are likewise numerous denominational places of worship. A workingman's reading and lecture rooms, which is liberally supported by the Countess Waldegrave and Lord Carlingford, and where refreshments and non-intoxicating drinks can be obtained has been established some years. As mentioned above, the North Somerset line has a station here. Very fine ales are brewed in Radstock and neighbourhood.

The station here will accommodate a somewhat wide and numerously populated district, Kilmersdon being one of the largest villages. The new line, like that of the North Somerset, has a level crossing here, the gates of both crossings being only about ten yards apart. The stations are also close together. The station-house is a pretty little building. There are two platforms and a goods shed. The level crossing gates are opened and closed by levers fixed in the signal-house, which contains thirty-one switch handles. Beneath the line is a subway formed by gradients on either side. This is for the convenience of carriages going to the station, and will also admit of the passage of vehicles when the gates are closed on account of passing trains.

RADSTOCK

From the S & D R Book of Rules and Regulations

At this station there is a Turnpike Road Level Crossing, and the gates are worked from the signal box. These gates must always be closed across the Turnpike Road before "Line Clear" is given to the next station.

A view across the heart of Radstock, c.1914. In the foreground is Ludlows Colliery with, behind it, the Waldegrave colliery workshops. Beyond again are the Somerset & Dorset station, the Waldegrave Arms, the tall brick chimney of Middle Pit and, on the horizon, the hill-top waste batches of Clandown Colliery. To the centre left is the Great Western station.

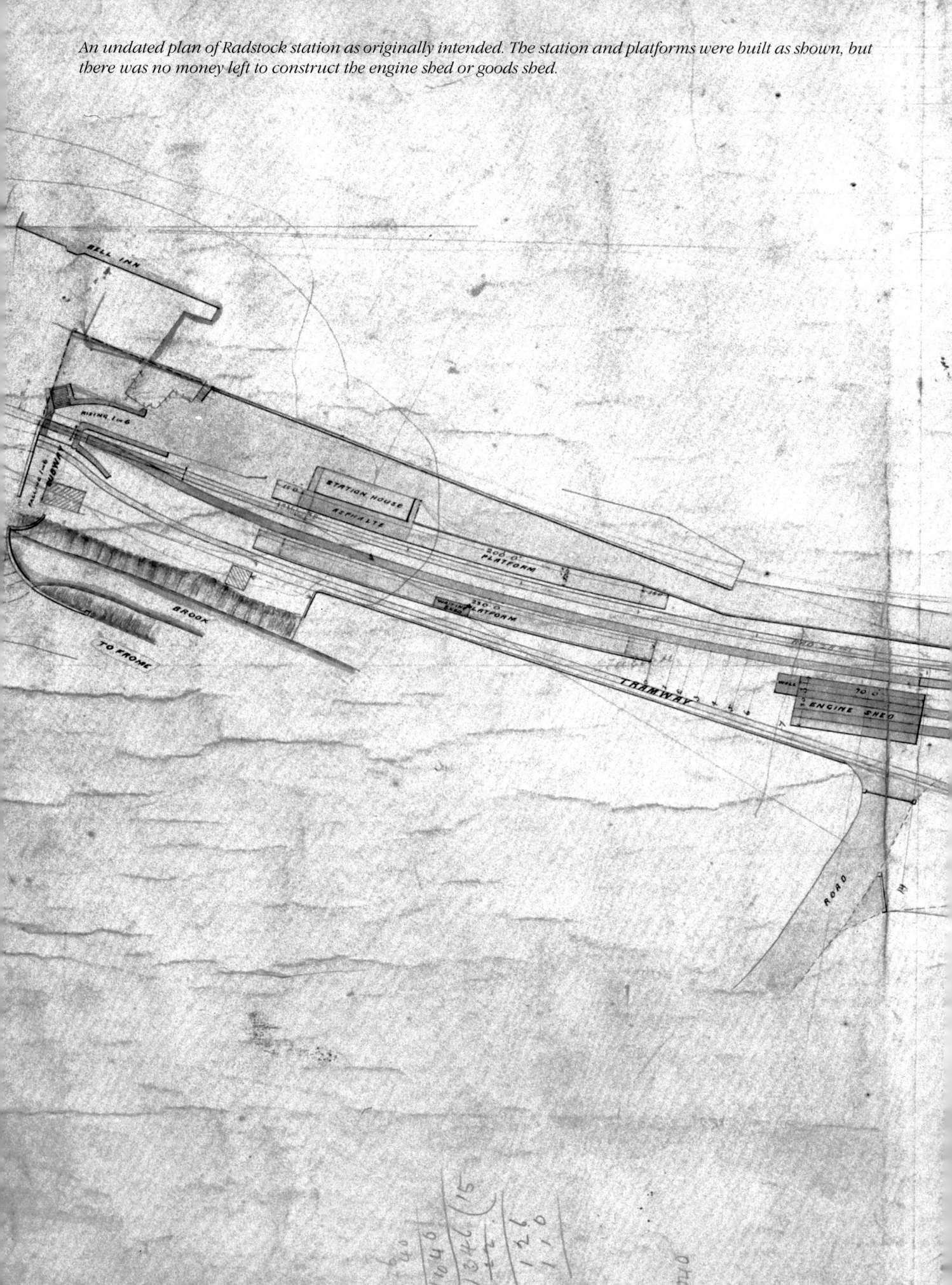
An undated plan of Radstock station as originally intended. The station and platforms were built as shown, but there was no money left to construct the engine shed or goods shed.

SOMERSET AND DORSET RAILWAY
PLAN OF
RADSTOCK STATION

SCALE 40 FT = 1 IN

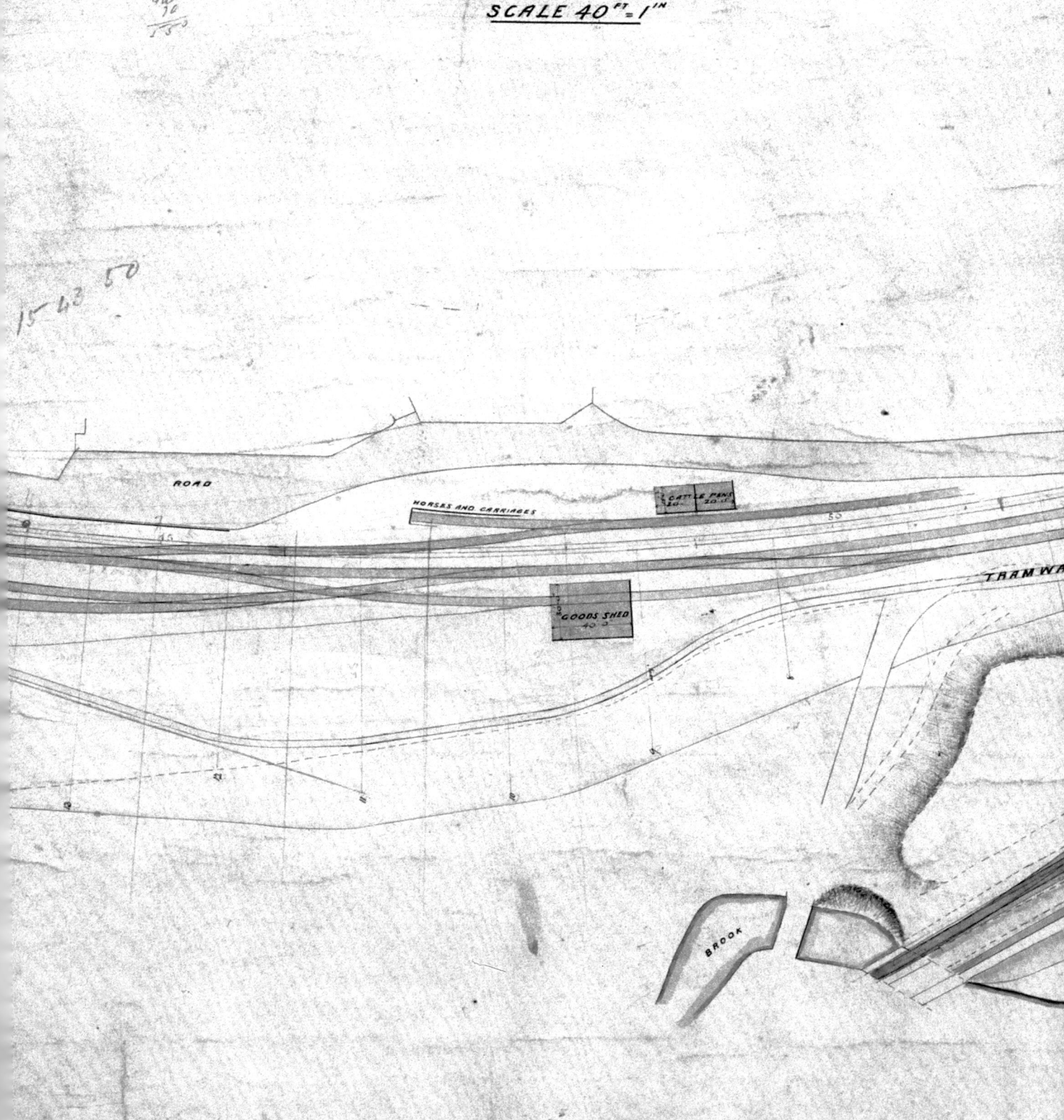

THE SOMERSET COAL FIELD

As this is the capital of the Somerset Coal Field, it will be interesting to give, at this point, a brief sketch of the geological and other features of the district. The information we shall give under this head is gained from a pamphlet written, in 1864, for the information of the British Association, the members of which visited the field during their congress in the city of Bath. The author of this little work was Mr Jas. MacMurtrie, the manager of the Countess Waldegrave's Radstock Collieries. He was guided and advised by Mr G.C. Greenwell, F.G.S.

The Somerset Coal Field extends from Bristol to the neighbourhood of Frome on the one hand and from the neighbourhood of Bath to the Mendip hills on the other. Its area is 150 square miles, but as the Bristol and Radstock districts are separated by an undeveloped tract, they are generally regarded as two fields.

Much obscurity exists respecting the early history of mining in the district. There are old records in the hands of the Waldegrave family which inform us that as early as the time of Edward IV, the lead mines of the Mendip Hills furnished employment for 10,000 miners, and the immense deposits of slags and slimes, found in the vicinity of Chewton Mendip, tell us of the early period of enterprise and industry; but, whether the fuel then used in smelting was obtained from the virgin forests of the country or raised from coal mines in the neighbouring valleys, is uncertain. Coal mining in this neighbourhood cannot probably lay claim to an antiquity so remote as the more northerly portion of the British coal field, but, judging from the known period at which it assumed a certain degree of importance in the district, we are inclined to think that contemporaneously, at all events with the lead mining period already referred to, coal was worked in the vicinity; and that in all probability, it has been carried on with a greater or less degree of activity for the last 400 years.

In the north-west and south portions the seams outcrop at the surface and here coal mining first took place; the appearances on the surface at Vobster, Nettlebridge, and Moorewood valleys tending to prove that coal was worked here at an early period, either by removing the surface or sinking shallow pits a short distance apart. At Paulton and Grayfield, where the seams are traceable along the surface, heaps of rubbish are thrown about so as to give probability to the theory that the coal was worked "opencast" before the introduction of mining proper.

At this time the existence of coal under Radstock was never dreamed of, and was even disputed. Coal, however, was found at Radstock by the sinking of a pit in 1763, and for the time the Old Pit was the wonder of the neighbourhood. Since then the working of coal at Radstock has steadily increased. The earliest means of raising coal seems to have been by horse drums and gins similar to those used at Box and Farleigh to draw blocks up the shafts of the freestone quarries. Two horses were used to do the work, and an ascending and descending skip or corve, made of a frame the sides of which were composed of iron pins, amidst which hazel twigs were wreathed, so as to hold the coal by a combination of iron and wicker-work, were used, the shafts being widened beyond the regulation 4½ feet, where they passed each other. In this way from 300 to 500 bushels of coal per day were raised, or about 20 tons per pit. When this system was in full operation there were 8 pits in the Nettlebridge district, 14 in Paulton district, and 7 in the Radstock district. Assuming that the quantity raised per day was 20 tons per pit, this would give a total output for the whole district of 580 tons per day, or 180,000 tons per year; but as in summer the pits were half idle, it is probable the total output did not exceed 14,000 tons per annum.

Water wheels were in several instances brought into use at a subsequent period for raising coal. Steam engines for drawing coals out of the pits were first introduced in the Radstock district about 70 years ago, and increased the output at the pits where they were used to 50 tons per day, which so recently as 1840 was considered a good day's work, so slowly did improvements take place. Seventy years ago some of the men were lowered and raised in a kind of box, and others were slung to the chains with nooses, in which they inserted their legs up to the thigh, clinging to the chain one above the other till there were 9 or 10.

The next improvement was the introduction of cages and guides similar but more rude than those now in use. From 1840 to 1850 the quantity drawn at individual pits increased but slowly. Only in one instance, and that by working night and day, was from 600 to 700 tons per week brought to bank, and probably 3,000 to 3,500 tons per week was the average production of every pit. From 1854 to 1864 immense strides in the way of improvement were made. Larger pits, more powerful and improved engines and cages were introduced at the Countess Waldegrave's pits.

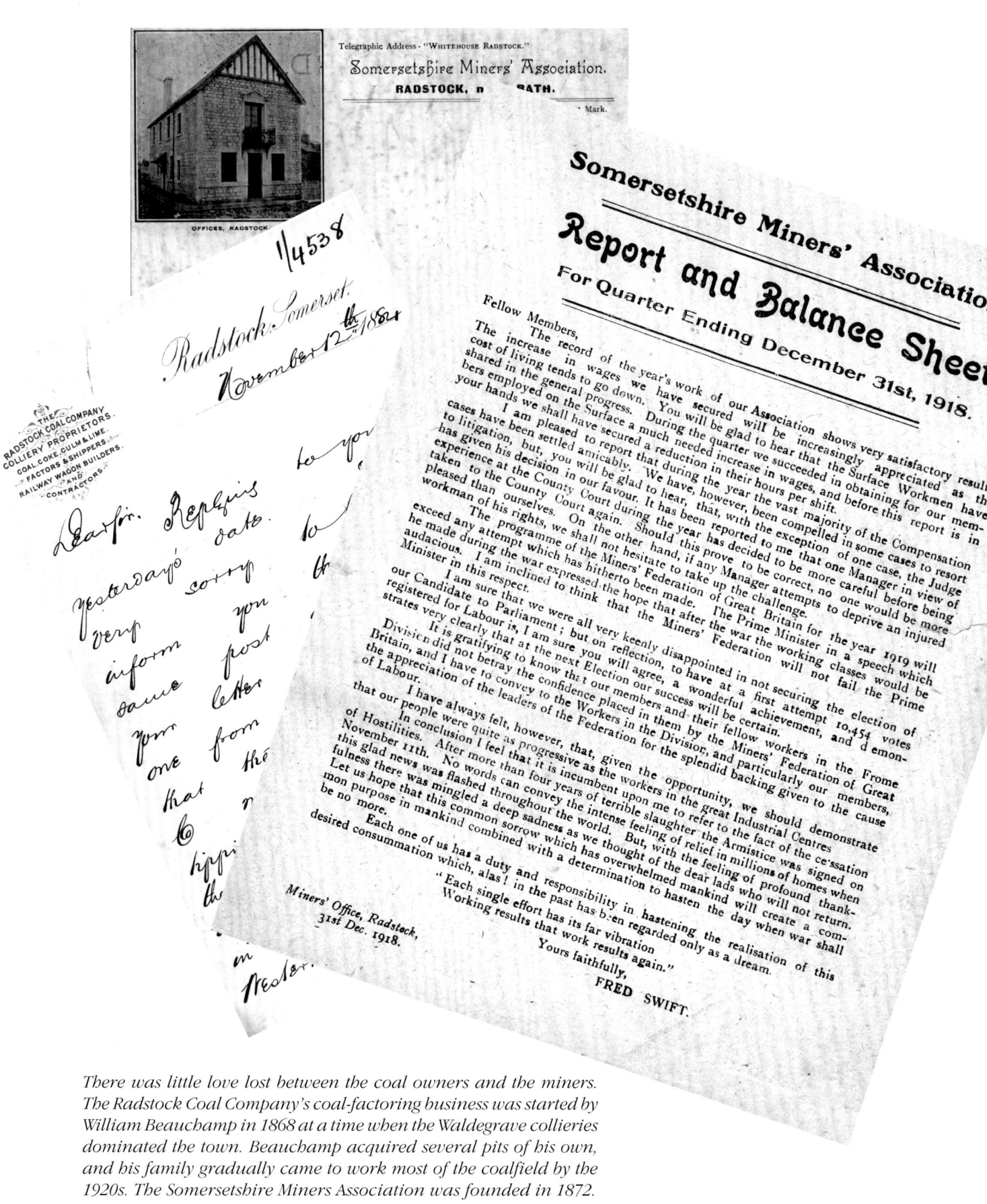

There was little love lost between the coal owners and the miners. The Radstock Coal Company's coal-factoring business was started by William Beauchamp in 1868 at a time when the Waldegrave collieries dominated the town. Beauchamp acquired several pits of his own, and his family gradually came to work most of the coalfield by the 1920s. The Somersetshire Miners Association was founded in 1872.

Other collieries soon followed the lead of her ladyship; but with all the improvements the quantities raised fall short of other districts. Owing to the upturned nature of the strata, the extreme thinness of the coal seams, and the great angle at which they lie, the district is not capable of that amount of improvement to be met with in more favoured coal fields. One great drawback is that the quantity of rubbish exceeds the storing room provided by the coal that is won, and thus it has to be hauled to bank at great cost. Notwithstanding these drawbacks as much as from 250 to 300 tons of coal and rubbish have been hauled from a single pit in a day. In the Radstock district there are now 13 pits, in the Paulton district a similar number, and in the Nettlebridge district 4.

New Rock Colliery, near Chilcompton. Coal mining on Mendip had begun in this area at least as early as the 15th Century. Down below New Rock in the Nettlebridge valley, Moorewood Colliery had been connected to the S&D by a rope incline and narrow gauge railway. Nearby Strap colliery was the destination of a branch line for which the S&D had obtained an Act in 1873, but which was never built. New Rock itself was never directly rail connected, but nevertheless at one time owned several main line coal wagons which were based at Moorewood sidings. This photograph was taken in 1968, shortly before the pit closed.

The total quantity does not probably exceed 600,000 tons per year, which compared with the quantity obtained seventy years ago, gives a balance for the present time of 460,000 tons per year.

The system of work adopted is that known as the "longwall," being the one most suited for the peculiarities of the field. The crush upon the roads is so great that they require constant enlargement. In the Vobster district where the coal is found in upright veins, the men take a slice several feet in thickness off the bottom and then repeat the operation as far as the vein runs up. The district is remarkably free from fire-damp, excepting in some fiery veins adjoining the Mendip Hills, which are worked at Newbury, Vobster and Edford. Three of the pits here are especially fiery. For geologists the neighbourhood of Radstock possesses many objects of singular interest. The coal measures are commonly overlaid by at least three formations, the oolite, lias, and red sandstone. In the lias quarries fossils, principally shells abound. A little magnesian limestone is also found. All these formations lie in a nearly horizontal position, and are scarcely at all disturbed by faults, proving that the period since their deposition has been one of comparative repose, denudation having apparently

done for this district what disclocation has done for others, and thus we have the numerous valleys to which Somerset owes so much of its picturesque beauty.

The coal measures lying immediately under the formations already alluded to, present a remarkable contrast to them. The period between their deposition and the age of the new red sandstone must have been one of much disturbance. Faults varying in depth from a foot to 100 fathoms traverse the field in all conceivable directions – the seams of coals being sometimes found level, sometimes vertical, and in others they have been turned upside down and folded over, rendering their mining a question of much difficulty and uncertainty. Where these peculiar overlapped faults stand, pits sunk on the points where they exist pass through them twice; therefore the geological structure of the district is somewhat complex.

The coal measures of the Radstock district consist of three divisions, the upper being termed the Radstock series, the second the Farrington, and the lower series. The upper series is worked in the vicinity of Radstock and Paulton, and consists of seven seams of coals, six of which, varying from 14 to 30 inches in thickness, are commonly workable. Between the lowest seam of this series to the highest of the Farrington series from ninety to 120 fathoms of strata intervene, a band of reddish shale, about 20 fathoms in thickness being the distinguishing division. The Farrington series, as proved at Norton-hill, consists of six seams varying from 18 to 36 inches in thickness, and three of them have been worked. Perhaps no coal field in the world produces so large a variety of well preserved fossil plants as the Radstock district. The theory of the curious overlap referred to above is that they were caused by lateral pressure, aided perhaps by the fact that the seams were then in a plastic state.

CLANDOWN ~ 1898

The easiest way to make an excursion to the principal coal field area of Somerset is to take the train from the Midland Station (S.D.R.) to Radstock, the centre of the mining industry, and from that place to visit some of the neighbouring pit parishes.

Or should some ardent pedestrian, cyclist, or charioteer, prefer the road to rail, let him take a bracing and invigorating journey along the Wells Road, past Odd Down, down Dunkerton Hill, and ascend Wellow Hill. Then in a straight course, by taking the first turn to the right, after leaving the entrance gates to Woodborough House on the left, the "jaded" traveller still going straight forward, lands on Clandown Common, commanding as it does, one of the finest outlooks of landscape in the county. For miles and miles the Mendip Hills stretch far and wide. The church of the Holy Trinity, and Clandown Colliery are situated, though in different directions, near to the top slope of the breezy down, and both are almost within a stone's throw of one another. The village lies below, and extends to the bottom of the hill. Most of the cottages are in possession of Mr William Ashman, who, now in his 87th year, was one of the first churchwardens appointed thirty years ago, and still acts in that capacity. Other tenements are owned by the Duchy of Cornwall. In addition to the colliery (which is the chief industry of the place), a brewery and coach-building establishment are the other principal places of business. The church and village have arisen mainly in consequence of mining operations, and not so many years ago Clandown was merely a scattered hamlet, situated as it is at present, within the civil parish of Midsomer Norton.

Leaving Radstock Station, a steep hill passing a disused shaft brings us to Clandown. The first object of interest is the gug, a steep railway incline, up and down which the wagons are pulled by a windlass. On one occasion the cord gave way, and the wagon rushed down the incline with such violence that it smashed everything in its course till it came to a standstill. Near this gug is a square of new houses erected for the colliers, formerly a tallow factory. Near here lives Mr William Ashman, who not only carried on this business, but in the old days before the railway was made between Radstock and Bath, used to carry all the coal down to the barges on the canal at Midford. His father was the first man to discover the presence of coal in this district, and it was by his advice the trial was made. The first dividend of this colliery was paid in 1815. In a garden of the square one of the old boilers is still to be seen. From his window the old Roman road is distinctly visible, and is of great interest to the antiquarian. It crosses the gug and goes to Ilchester. At the top of the gug we come to the coal pit, which I contemplated going down, but when I saw the dense smoke coming out of the pit's mouth I said, "No thank you."

The colliery is one of the oldest and best known in the Somerset mining area, and has been in operation about 90 years. At the present time six veins of the Upper or Radstock Series, having a total thickness of 11 feet, are being worked, yielding coal celebrated

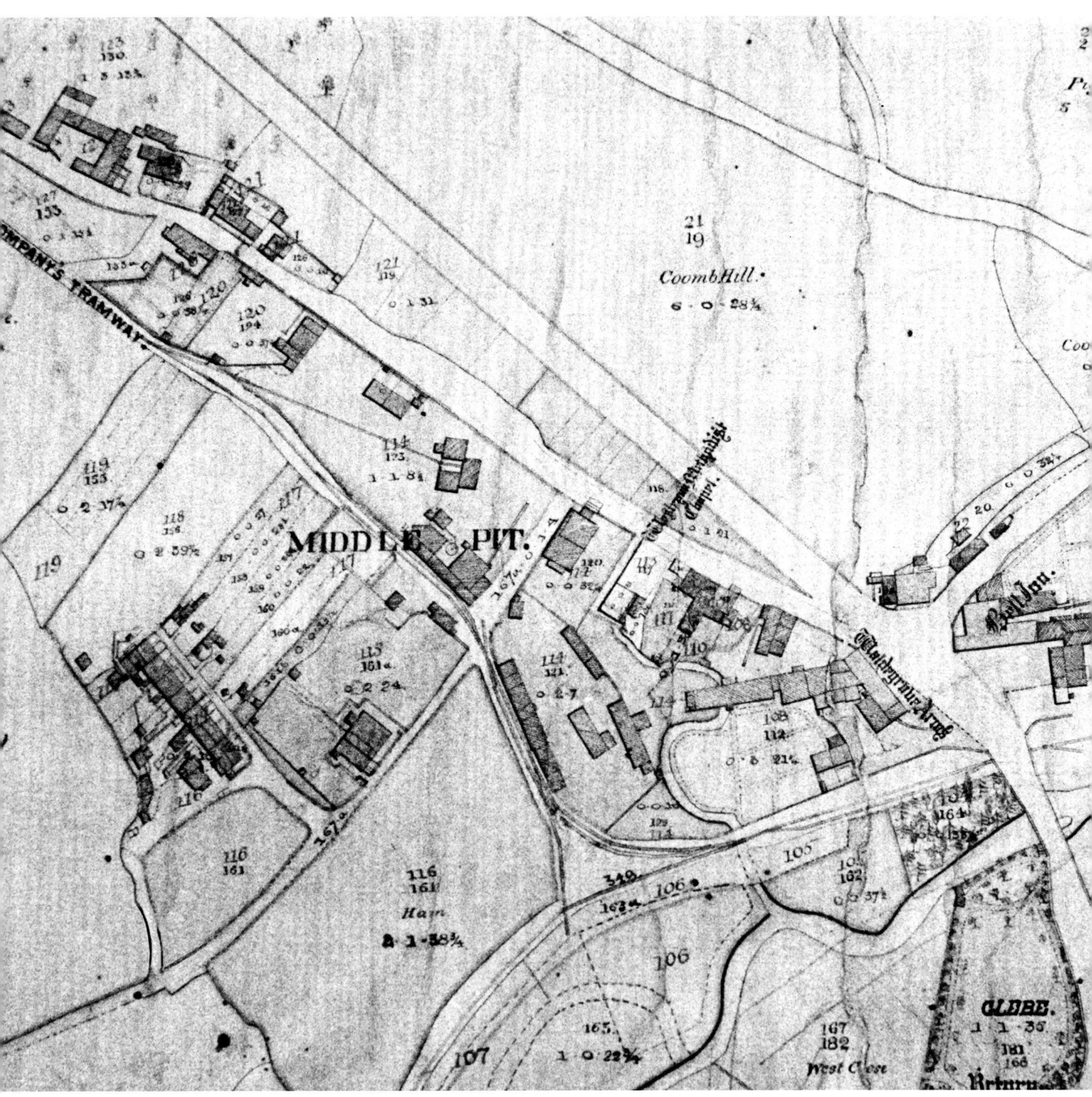

This map of Radstock, c.1860, shows the Coal Canal tramway weaving under the main road (using the old canal bridge) past the Waldegrave Arms, then forking north towards Middle Pit and Clandown, and west towards Welton.

for house, gas, and steam purposes. Many years ago the largest portion of the product was conveyed by horses over the tramway to Midford, where it was loaded into boats and shipped by the canal to Bath and other places. When the Great Western Railway Company opened a branch line from Frome to Radstock, canal shipments were discontinued, and the coal was taken to Radstock and there loaded into railway trucks. Still more recently [in 1882] the colliery has been directly connected by means of *a branch line with the Somerset and Dorset Railway, and the company's own trucks are loaded at the pit's mouth.*

The property is owned by the Duchy of Cornwall, and leased, together with the Old Welton and Welton Hill Collieries, having a total of 1,170 acres, by the Trustees of the late F. Bird, Esq., of Norton House.

There are two shafts at the Clandown Colliery, one for hoisting and the other for pumping purposes, and are each nearly 500 yards deep. They are situate about one mile from Radstock, and eight miles from Bath, and correspond nearly with the centre of the coal basis. The sinking was commenced in the lower beds of the inferior oolite, passing through the lias and new red sandstone, and then penetrating the coal measures. Owing to the fact that the pits are exactly on the line of the great north and south fault of the district, which has a vertical throw of 120 fathoms, the coals were not met with for a long distance, the lower part of the shafts being on the downthrow of the fault. The dip of the measure is about nine inches per yard north-east.

The underground workings are very extensive, horses being used for haulage purposes, but the owners are at the present time making improvements with the view of introducing rope haulage and steam power, which will do the work horses are now doing, and greatly increase the output of the colliery, which has sufficient coal in the Upper Series of veins alone to last another half-century. Before the cage was used for bringing miners up the shaft a "gus" was employed. Batches of men were raised by means of a chain affixed to a rope which supported their bodies. The "gus" with its living freight strongly resembled a string of onions.

The colliers formerly descended the pit on Sunday night, but this is happily the case no longer. The time for descending the pit is 4.45 am, and work commences for all at 6 am; the day shift coming up at 1 pm and the boys at 3 pm. The night shift descends at 7 pm and comes up at 5 am.

Clandown coal is bituminous, durable, and gas producing, and has supplied the Bath Gas Company for many years with considerable supplies.

The Vicar speaks well of the musical powers of his Choir, which for the most part are connected with the collieries. Anthems and Cathedral Services are sung with considerable precision and the services are fully choral. This is all the more remarkable when it is remembered that the services rendered are gratuitous, and the members of his congregation are poor labouring people in a struggling colliery parish.

RADSTOCK *to* EVERCREECH

Leaving the Radstock market-place we pass along the line and notice that it runs by the side of the tramway from Wellsway and Old Welton Pits. A siding is being constructed up to Wellsway pit for the benefit of the North Somerset Railway. This line is crossed about 200 yards from Radstock by a five-arched viaduct which is substantially built. Only one line of rails at present exists but the chief arch has at the request of the company been made to accommodate two lines and an extra arch is provided for another line, which is very much in prospect. Adjoining this viaduct is one of the heaviest embankments on the line. It crosses Welton Bottom and underneath it runs a spacious culvert 120 feet long for the brook flowing down the valley and a bridge through which the Midsomer Norton road passes. This bridge is brick built. The walls run up to a short distance only and then the arch springs off, this plan being considered in this instance more safe than high walls with heavy masses of earth pressing against it on either side.

The Wells Way Pit, also belonging to her ladyship, is on the south side up a steep incline, but is hardly observable; a good view of the works at the Welton and Welton-hill pits is however obtained. Moving onwards, an excellent view of Midsomer Norton is presented and a small iron girder bridge, from which the residence of Mrs Savage may be seen, having been crossed, the train arrives at the station, 12½ miles from Bath.

Midsomer Norton is a large, pretty populous, and compactly built village. The North Somerset railway has a station near the village. There are five collieries and several large breweries in the parish and these supply a large amount of employment. The church is a handsome edifice of modern gothic design. There is a large market-hall and a well built bank here. The station is close to the place and there will be a goods shed here also. A great deal of business is done at Midsomer Norton as it is surrounded by a considerable agricultural area and does not partake so entirely of the colliery element as several other places in the district. A clear brook meanders through the place which stands amidst fertile fields the attractiveness of which is considerably augmented by a plenitude of handsome trees. Stratton-on-the-Fosse an ancient hamlet is a short distance to the south-east and this and other outlying places will be accommodated by the railway here.

The photograph above shows the station staff at Midsomer Norton, caught in its prime in the summer of 1899. Below is the signalman's view. The year is 1968 and, although the windows are broken, the station is still pretty much as it was left two years before, silent but intact.

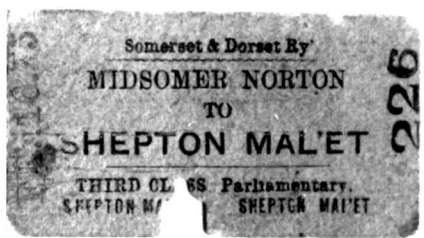

Leaving Midsomer Norton the train enters Chilcompton cutting, which is 44 feet deep and nearly half a mile long. It runs through a strata of white lias, a black stratum rich in phosphate of lime, red marl and grey lias. Passing through a short tunnel, over an embankment on a curve, from which Chilcompton is well seen, and through a cutting of red and yellow sand stone conglomerate, chiefly composed of limestone breccia, or "plum-pudding stone," the train stops at Chilcompton station, 14½ miles from Bath.

Two or three kinds of rocks and clay are met with in the Chilcompton cutting, and when the sun is shining on the different strata their aspect from the variety of colours is kaleidoscopic. The plan adopted throughout the line of boring a preliminary tunnel large enough for trucks to enter and then sinking small shafts which were made to act as funnels until the whole of the material around them had been thrown into the trams below, was here resorted to. This cutting, like the others, entailed a great deal of labour, which, however, was economised by the mode just described. Near the station is another cutting of conglomerate or pudding stone, so-called from the medley of shells and material of which it is composed. This cutting, from the intense toughness of the stone, was one of the most difficult sections of the work met with during the undertaking. The most destructive gunpowder was found futile in blasting it, and dynamite, a far more powerful explosive had to be used. To use dynamite is extremely ticklish work, and only the foreman navvies were allowed to handle it.

Nearly the whole of the navvies employed on the line have left the district, and the temporary huts which were erected for their accommodation are now only sparsely tenanted. It was curious, however, to notice the interest with which the few navvies and labourers flattered themselves that such a consummation was in no small measure due to their exertions. One solitary navvy was to be seen outside a hut, and his attitude and appearance irresistibly created a mental reminiscence of a reading acquaintance with the "Last of the Mohicans."

In another place an old navvy left the train with a huge bundle containing, amongst other things, a set of tin cooking apparatus, and addressing the guard called out "Well; the Lord bless you, guard, and prosper your new line." After having thus canonically blessed the undertaking, on which he said he had worked two years, he slipped the bundle over his shoulder, and remarking that he had to walk a distance of 17 miles and he hadn't seen his wife for a year, commenced his pilgrimage.

Below the station is a pretty wooded gorge, running down to the village, which is especially attractive, possessing as it does many permanent beauties – a limpid brook with charming waterfalls at short intervals, and such a handsome grotto spring as is seldom seen, besides sylvan treasures in abundance, the rich foliage of which shades the main road. Chilcompton will also possess a goods station.

Stratton and Downside are adjacent places, and the extensive Roman Catholic seat of learning known as Downside College will contribute many passengers to the line. Indeed this educational establishment isolated as it hitherto has been from railways will especially feel the convenience of the line, the nearest station until recently being Shepton Mallet seven, and Bath 14 miles. The College, which possesses an observatory, is a large building, and its size has recently been increased. It is sometimes thrown open to the public. At present Mr Bladwell, of Bath, is engaged in erecting a church in connection with the college. Oakhill too, with its noted breweries, is nearly as close to this station, as that at Shepton Mallet, and the large brewery at Holcombe is near at hand. We should imagine that whilst a considerable circuit in this district will be benefited by the line, it in turn will receive a large amount of support, as the run to Bath will be only thirteen miles, or about half-an-hour's journey.

Shortly after leaving Chilcompton a brief distance of light work speedily terminates in a lengthy cutting in mountain limestone overlaid by soil, situate at Old Down of coaching renown. The village of Chilcompton nestles beneath the northern slope of the Mendips and after passing that village we commence the passsage over the Mendips.

Gurney Slade, a mile and a half from Chilcompton, there is a station, and as the mountain limestone is extensively quarried here for road-repairing purposes a considerable amount of traffic may accrue from this point. Near the village of Gurney Slade, which is situate in a sequestered and romantic dell watered by a rivulet, is a heavy limestone cutting and a viaduct of six arches. From this structure there is a good view.

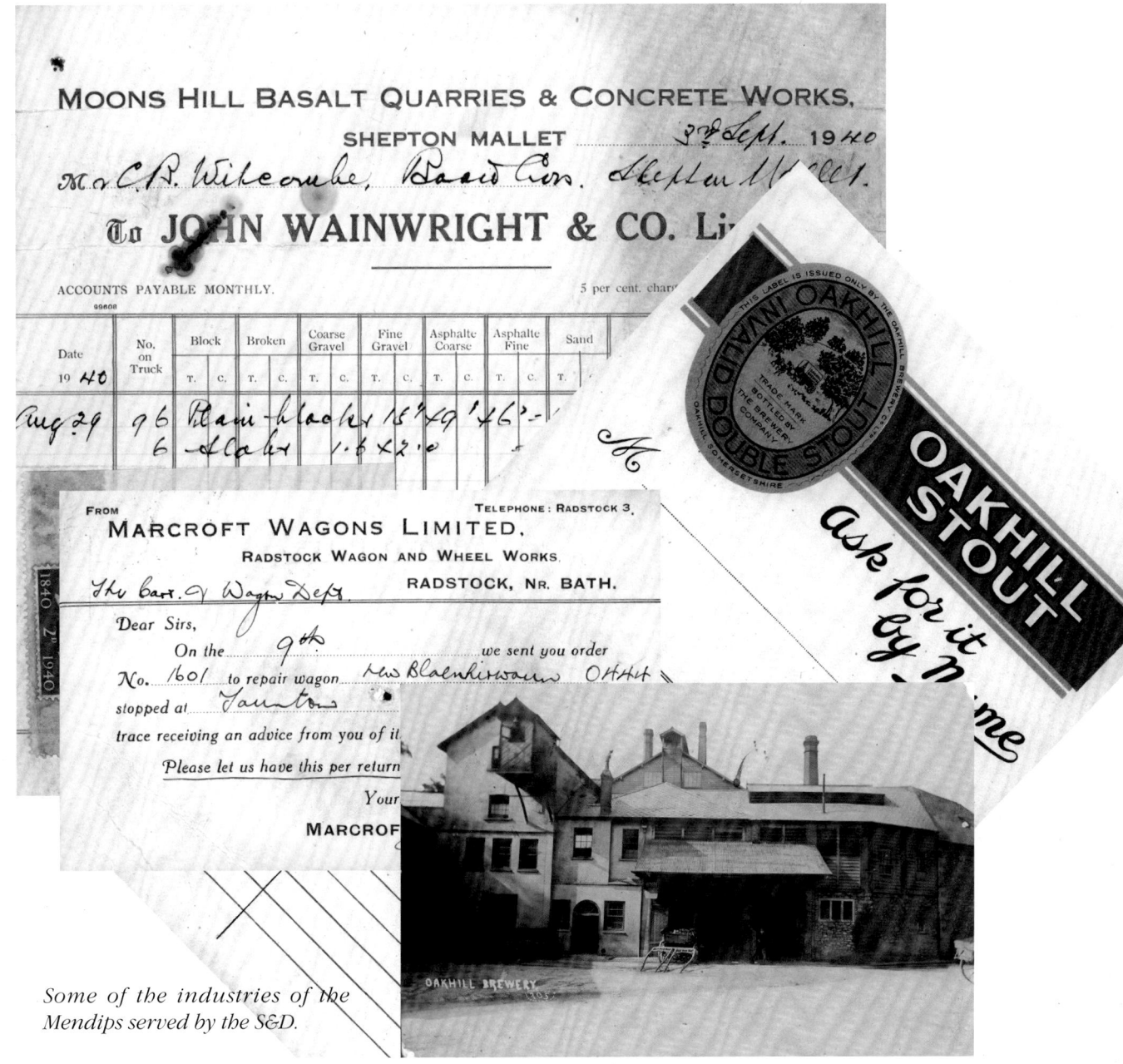

Some of the industries of the Mendips served by the S&D.

[Gale's reference to a "station" at Gurney Slade is curious. It is possible that even at this early stage, there was a quarry siding and wharf here, 1½ miles from Chilcompton and north of the six-arch Nettlebridge viaduct. As Gale says, there was extensive quarrying in the vicinity, and sidings here eventually served several other industrial concerns. It became better known as Moorewood.]

We believe that the line is taken across the Mendips at a low point, but the work all up the northern slope, although not so deep as might have been expected, has been difficult from the hardness of the limestone rock which is met with just beneath the soil. As we approach the Mendips the strata which overlie the coal deposits are lost and others supervene, hence the existence of the comglomerate, mountain, and magnesian limestone at various points. A noticeable feature of the landscape is that after leaving Radstock we lose sight of the numerous hills and valleys which characterise the district between Bath and Radstock and come into larger and broader valleys which in turn disappear on approaching the Mendip range, the northern slope of which is agreeably diversified by woods and trees amongst which oak predominates.

Binegar station is reached at 17 miles. Here there was a flag flying, and in an adjacent field a red banner of considerable size had been fixed, whereon, in large white letters, were the words "Success to the Railway." The station is exactly opposite the village of Binegar, the church of which stands high and exposed on the Mendip range. From this point the view Bathward is delightful. Binegar church has a fine tower with panelled embattlements. A large horse fair, the biped and quadruped attendance of which will annually increase the traffic of the line, is held here. The Binegar horse fair is still one of the largest and most important in the west of England for draught and other classes of animals. It is a well-known fact that the spread of railways has tended to make markets grow in importance and fairs decline. This has been in a modified degree the case at Binegar, but the existence of a railway will perhaps revive it to the pitch at which it once stood.

Near this village stands an eminence, one of those "beacon hills" which are immortalized in Macaulay's stirring poem of "The Armada." This beacon is 1,020 feet above the sea and is the highest eminence on the eastern division of the range. Regardless of natural impediments the Fosse Way was carried across this eminence, whilst the modern road shirks it, and thus there are afforded instances of ancient persistence and modern expediency.

Shortly after, the Mendip range is entered and the train proceeds through the Maesbury cutting. This is the "pass" by which the line crosses the Mendip hills, and is therefore the highest point of the railway, being 800 feet above the level of the Midland Railway terminus at Bath. The cutting is long, runs through the inferior oolite, and is 40 feet deep.

We speedily arrive at Maesbury Station, so named from the fact that an ancient encampment stands on an eminence a short distance away. It was at first proposed to call this station Dinder, the village of that name being in the neighbourhood, but at the suggestion of Mr Lovell, who owns the land and whose coat of arms surmounts the station-master's house which it was found necessary to build, it was named Maesbury. [The railway always spelt it "Masbury".] The encampment, which is of British origin, is in a good state of preservation. It stands amongst trees, and has a double ring of earthworks. The camp encloses six acres and must have occupied a formidable position. The encampment stands on the line of the Roman road along the crest of the hill from the Bristol Channel to Old Sarum. We are now on the summit of the Mendips.

Leaving Maesbury, we commence the descent of the Mendips and, passing through a pleasant country, come to Ham-hill Viaduct [Ham Wood viaduct] of six arches. The viaduct crosses a beautiful wooded glen, a branch of which runs some distance beside the line, whilst the uplands around are dotted by copses and timber. Another mile, and to the west of the line, there is unfolded one of the most glorious panoramas of English scenery which it has ever been our fortune to behold. We are now on the southern slope of the Mendip range, and looking away in a south-westerly direction a wide expanse of flat country, standing prominently amidst which is Glastonbury Tor, rising like a giant above the surrounding landscape.

As the eye surveys the expansive district other less prominent tumuli come within optical ken, and anon the view is shut out by another range of hills rising indistinctly to the sky line. The town of Glastonbury, with its Abbey and other places, are included in the scene. Our glance at this unrivalled prospect is of short duration, as we speedily come under the shadow of an eminence which is an offshoot of the Mendips. This is tunneled; hard mountain limestone being the rock found, to conquer which dynamite was used. From the fact that the veins of stone are almost upright in places brick lining is occasionally used. [This was Winsor Hill tunnel, during construction of which four labourers had been killed by a rock fall the previous summer, on 18th August 1873. The railway always called it Winsor Hill rather than Windsor Hill which is the usual local spelling.]

At the foot of this hill stands the town of Shepton Mallet, which we catch sight of on emerging from the tunnel. The Bath-road viaduct, a mile further on is the finest viaduct on the line. There are six arches of 50 feet span rising 62 feet above the road. From this viaduct, which from the road below presents a very fine and substantial appearance, a good view is obtained of the church and town of Shepton Mallet. [I suspect that Gale intended to compliment Charlton Road viaduct as the finest on the line, not Bath Road.]

Continuing the curve round the town by means of the Charlton viaduct, consisting of 27 arches of 30 feet span and nearly 50 feet high, the train draws up at the Shepton Mallet station, which is nearly half a mile from the centre of the town, and about 22 miles from Bath.

Shepton Mallet is a town of considerable commercial importance both in an agricultural and manufacturing sense. The contractors' offices at this end have been situate here. The Great Western Railway has a station here. Shepton Mallet is a town of nearly 6000 inhabitants.

When in the reign of Queen Elizabeth [I] additional impetus was given to the West of England cloth trade by the passing of an Act forbidding the exportation of wool, Shepton whose position under the Mendips made it a prolific wool producing district, became a great cloth manufacturing centre; but the introduction of machinery in the north and its long isolation from railways caused the trade to decline. In later years its trade has revived and velvet and crepe making, brick and pottery works, beside large breweries, and the manufacturing of wearing apparel usually purchased in an important agricultural town make Shepton Mallet a busy place.

There is a very fine parish church which has an attractive aspect when regarded from a distance, and it by no means suffers on closer inspection. There are likewise in the town an ancient market cross, elaborately worked, a literary institution and reading-room, a mechanics institute, grammar school, handsome Roman Catholic Chapel, almshouses and denominational chapels. There is an extensive market-place where a market is held on Fridays and where many first-class agricultural products are bartered. Bowlish, Charlton, Cannard's-grave, and Oakhill, where are the celebrated breweries for the widely renowned stout and beer, are close at hand, and the latter village, which is three miles distant, will send much traffic to the line. At Doulting, two miles west of the town, there are

The northern entrance to the original 242-yard long Winsor Hill tunnel. The photograph dates from 1891/2 when a second, shorter tunnel was built to accommodate the up main line. To the left is Winsor Hill stone quarry siding, opened in 1875 and controlled by the little wooden signal box on the right. When the double line was opened, this early box was replaced by a solid stone one sited slightly to the north.

The gracefulness of the original single track viaducts on the Bath Extension is exemplified in this view of Charlton Road Viaduct at Shepton Mallet, taken when the first stages of widening were in progress in 1891.

Last respects are paid at Shepton Mallet on 6th March 1966. The southbound SLS special train hauled by 2-8-

numerous extensive quarries, where excellent stone is produced, and from which came the stone for building portions of Wells Cathedral, Glastonbury Abbey, and several other ecclesiastical structures in the neighbourhood. The stone greatly resembles our Bath oolite blocks but is harder. No doubt additional railway accommodation will further develop the quarries.

At Shepton Mallet Station, which is about a quarter of a mile from the town, there will also be a commodious goods shed. Just beyond the station is Cannard's Grave cutting, a mile and a quarter long, cut through the lias, the rock being very hard and full of fossils and 45 feet deep. [When the line was doubled, the excavations in 1887 to widen the cutting dug into and destroyed the remains of a substantial Roman building.] The cutting runs beneath the East Somerset

No 48706 and 2-6-4T No 80043 pauses for breath and a photocall after its climb over Masbury Summit.

line, and there are strong occupation bridges across it. At the end of the cutting a heavy embankment, two miles long commences, and, in the centre of it is Prestleigh Viaduct, another imposing structure of eleven arches. We are now getting close to Doulting-hill, an eminence of considerable height and on which numerous flocks of sheep browse. Hard by is the Evercreech Village station, shortly after which the line joins the parent system. Evercreech, which is an ancient and well appointed village, will benefit considerably by the line, which supplies it with a station at a distance of a quarter of a mile, whilst the old Evercreech and Ditcheat station was a mile and-a-half away.

To meet the expected requirements of additional traffic, further station buildings and offices are being erected at Evercreech [Junction].

Somerset & Dorset Railway – Bath Extension.

Dr. Michell's Land at Evercreech.

In connection with Severance it is evident that in consequence of the insufficient headway of the Arch under the existing S. & D. Railway the only means of transit of a load from one part of the Estate to another must be over the line at the level Crossing; and from the default of the Railway Company in not carrying out the 12 feet headway as agreed by the Contract of 1858 the evil of another level Crossing over the Bath Extension is again forced upon this Estate –

A level Crossing is dangerous under any circumstance but in this case the danger is greatly increased in consequence of the two Railways being so close together as to create a distance of 47 yards which must be passed over before a Cart or Waggon could get clear of both lines of Railway – This danger is also aggravated by the Extension Line being on a sharp curve at this spot and passing immediately into a Cutting 20 feet deep so that the approach of a Train from the North could not be observed from the East side of the Railway, the natural rise of the ground also preventing a more distant view of an approaching Train –

The Junction of the two Railways at this spot increases the danger and inconvenience very seriously, as any irregularity of the Trains on the Somerset & Dorset Railway, which is a single Line, would cause a stoppage on the Extension Railway, and as a large heavy traffic is expected to come upon the latter very great inconvenience might be caused to a Tenant at any time but more especially during Hay Harvest when quick carrying to the Rick is of importance –

There cannot be a doubt that the fee simple value of this Property will be very greatly diminished by the future singularly bad access to it and which must be permanent –

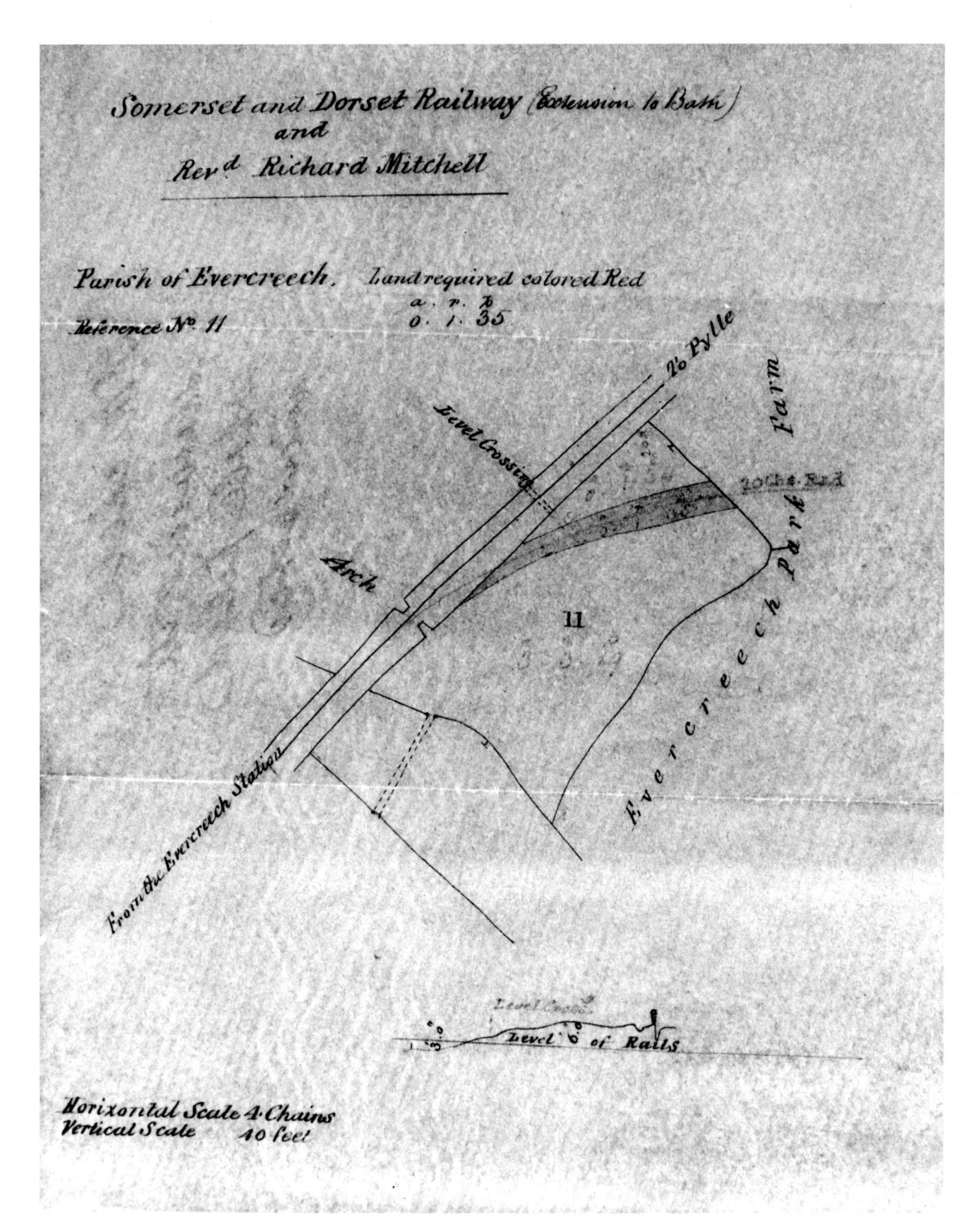

The plan above shows a plot of land at Evercreech which the S&D intended to purchase from Rev Dr Mitchell in 1872 in order to construct the junction between the Bath Extension and the orignal Burnham-Wimborne line. Negotiations for the purchase were complicated. The railway company had built an arch beneath the original line to allow access from one side to the other, but it was smaller than agreed. Consequently the tenant farmer who occupied the fields on either side was using a level crossing instead, and would now need another to cross the new line. The problem is outlined in the document shown opposite. Whereas the actual land needed for the new railway was valued at £45, a compensation claim for all the inconvenience was made for £270.

EVERCREECH JUNCTION
From the S & D R Book of Rules and Regulations

From the Junction with the Old Line to Evercreech Old Station the Line is doubled, and the Signals are arranged accordingly.

SPEED OF TRAINS THROUGH STATIONS & JUNCTIONS

Trains running through the loop at the Stations where they are not timed to stop, must not run over the Loop at a higher speed than 10 miles an hour.

No Train must run over the Junctions at Evercreech and Bath at a greater speed than 10 miles an hour.

WHISTLES

In approaching and leaving Evercreech Junction two distinct whistles must be given with the small whistle.

A large number of persons in addition to intending travellers were here and also at Wincanton to see the first down train from Bath, which, after delays at both places, contrived to reach Temple Combe, the junction with the London and South Western Railway, after their down train for Exeter had departed. So the poor passengers going west, instead of reaching Exeter at 11.53 had to wait for the next train. This was very late, so that instead of reaching the Devonshire capital at 1.20, it did not arrive there till five minutes to two. This is a bad beginning. May the Somerset and Dorset managers speedily "mend their ways" in the matter of puntuality, or they will only too quickly find that would-be travellers will go by their longer yet fairly punctual competitors, rather than by a route where times of arrival are uncertain and delays not improbable, albeit the mileage may be considerably less.

PUNCTUALITY OF TRAINS
From the S & D R Book of Rules and Regulations

Safety and efficiency in working to a large extent depends on the punctuality of the Train Service, and this depends on the promptitude and activity used at the several stations in despatching trains. The particular attention of the Station Agents must be invariably given to this, and they will be held strictly responsible for the work at their respective stations, and they must report to the Traffic Superintendent all cases of neglect or inability on the part of their staff.

"Here we are detained for hours owing to the lateness of the Somerset & Dorset trains ... I don't know when we shall get to Charmouth for we just hear that the South Western train is very late. However we must put up with it."
[This was written by Thomas Bennett of Bruton to his father, in a letter posted at Templecombe, dated 11 o'clock on the 21st July, the day after opening.]

Throughout the week the trains have continued to run, but there have been, in some cases, a want of punctuality. Having to work in connection with three lines perhaps the Somerset and Dorset Railway is a difficult one, but we are assured that with a little more experience all the punctuality desirable will be attained.

We may add, that all who have ridden over the line have admired the beauty and variety of the scenery which distinguishes the route, and all the passengers with whom we have come in contact have expressed surprise at the smoothness of the new line.

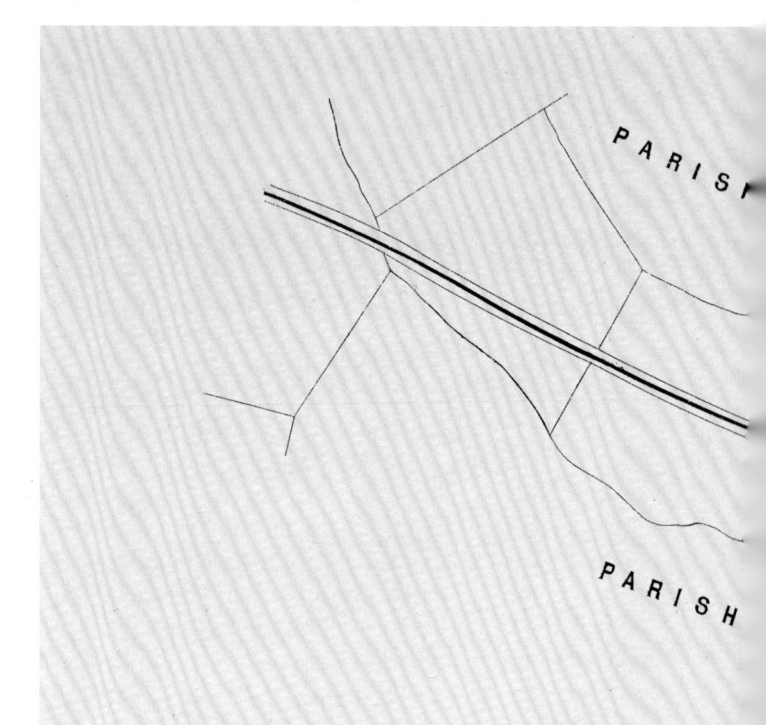

Classic Somerset & Dorset. S&DJR 2-8-0 No 53806 stands at Evercreech Junction, taking water before heading south on 18th August 1962. The 1864 plan below shows the site of the original 'Evercreech Old Station'.

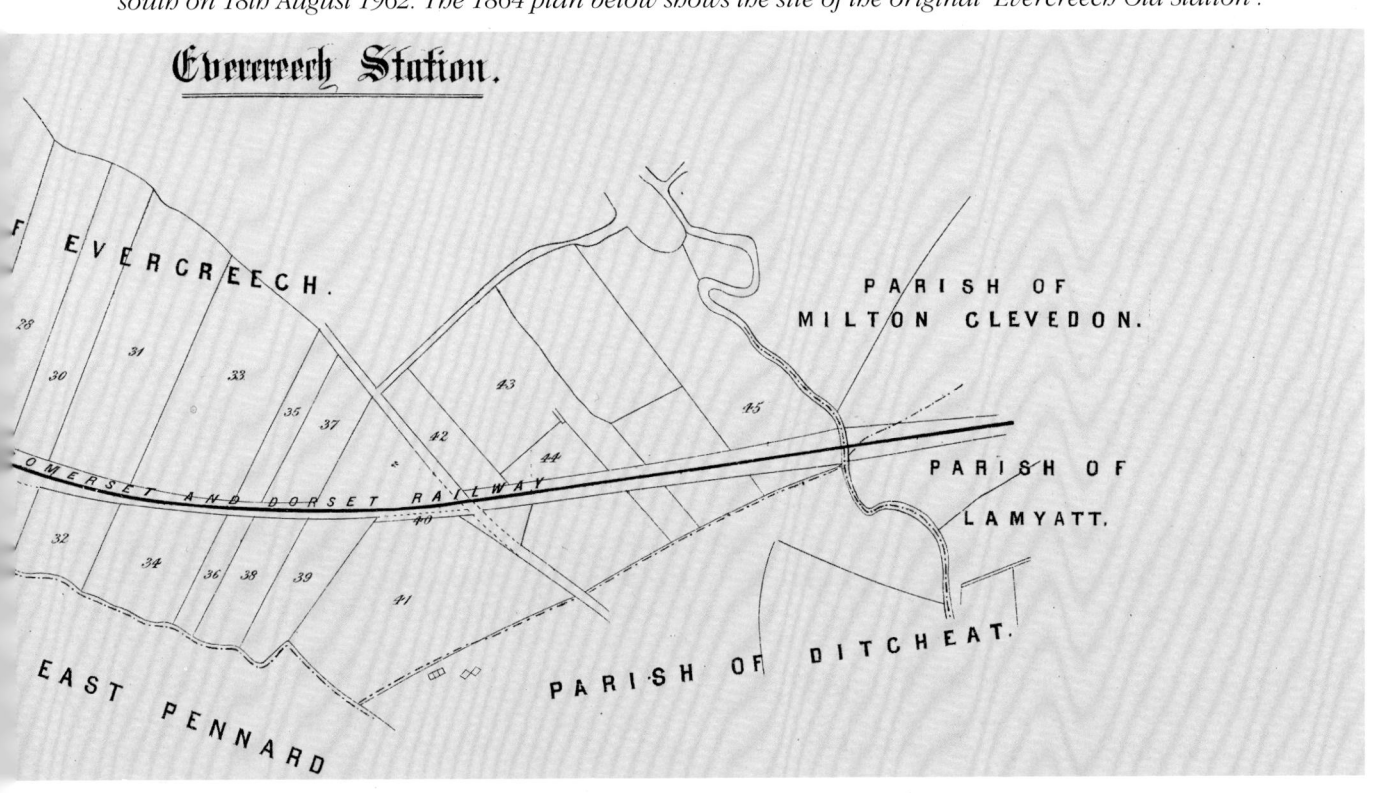

Important Sale of Contractor's Plant

Somerset & Dorset Railway Extension

MESSRS FULLER, HORSEY, SON and CO are instructed by Messrs T. and C. Walker to SELL by AUCTION on TUESDAY AUGUST 11th and following days at 1 precisely each day, at the depots, Bath, Radstock, and Shepton Mallet, all stations on the Somerset and Dorset Railway Extension, the CONTRACTOR'S PLANT, Stores, &c, lately used in the construction of the line, including four 6-wheel coupled inside cylinder saddle tank locomotive engines 4ft 8½ in gauge, two by Manning, Wardle and Co, and one by Worcester Engine Company; one outside cylinder ditto by Fox, Walker and Co; one 4-wheeled coupled inside cylinder locomotive engine by Appleby Brothers, a set of six spare wheels and axles with steel tires for Manning, Wardle and Co's engines, and 8-horse power traction engine by Aveling and Porter, and four road trollies, a 5-horse power ditto, with extra set of wheels to run on rails, seven portable steam engines from 5 to 10 horse power by Clayton and Shuttleworth and Ruston and Proctor; two vertical engines and boilers combined, 2½ and 4 horse power by Appleby Brothers and Ruston and Proctor; 200 end-tip earth waggons on wrought and cast iron wheels 4ft 8½ in gauge, 40 flat ballast waggons, 30 saddle back ballast waggons, 40 spring ballast waggons, 100 earth waggons 3ft gauge, about 300 tons contractors' rails from 20 to 54 lbs; five cast-iron mortar mills with pans 7ft and 7ft 6in diameter, four circular saw benches, will take in saws from 36in to 48in diameter, 8½-inch centre self-acting slide lathe, saw sharpening machine, four weighing machines from five cwt to one ton, seven double and single purchase crabs and winches, three cranes, powerful locomotive drug, six strong drugs for timber or rails, 21 two and one horse carts, 40 dobbin carts, two light spring carts, dog cart, pony cart, four-wheel phaeton, 45 sets of harness, about 250 navvy barrows, 40 pairs waggon wheels and axles, two tons wrought waggon work, a general assortment of stores comprising blocks and falls, lifting jacks, adze hammers, sledge and hand hammers, rope, smith's tools &c, about 27 tons wrought and cast scrap iron, 8½ tons bar iron, about seven tons nails, spikes and brobs, 2½ tons chain and chain slings, three tons platelayers' tools, 28cwt anvils, 25cwt cast iron swage blocks.

The Burleigh steam rock drill, 4,000 feet run 1½ and one inch wrought iron gas pipe in lengths, about 6,000 feet run wheeling planks, 5,000 feet run scaffold poles, 700 feet cube Memel timber, 1,500 shoring boards, 30 platelayers' tools, chests, several thousand fir sleepers, 150 fathoms firewood, about 130 loads useful timber bridge centring, ladders, trestles &c, six hand pumps, iron and wood water tanks, four chaffcutting machines, circular saws, stocks, dies, vices, benches, leather bands, forges and bellows, timber erections of sheds and stores, and numerous other Effects.

18 useful Cart Horses, 6 Nag Horses, Brougham, 2 Stanhopes, Waggonette, Phaeton, 2 four-wheel Dog Carts, 3 light Driving Carts, Harness, Saddles, Bean and Oat Crushers, Stable Fittings &c.

May be Viewed two working days previous and mornings of Sale, and Catalogues, 6d each, had at the various depots; and of Messrs FULLER, HORSEY, SON and CO, 11 Billiter Square, London, E.C.

Contractors manoeuvre the timber-framed centring for one of the arches during the reconstruction of Tucking Mill Viaduct at Midford in 1891.

*The final shadows fall across
Bath Green Park station,
5th March 1966.*

Cover photograph: The S&D at Radstock, c.1914. The double main line snakes through the town, the rear trucks of a Bath-bound goods train trailing over the level crossing. The tramway to Clandown and Welton, which ran from the goods yard and down behind the station, emerges from under the main line into the foreground but is by now out of use. The branch leading off to the left serves Middle Pit, the Gas Works and Clandown colliery.

*Published in 1998 by Millstream Books, 18 The Tyning, Bath BA2 6AL
Set in Garamond and printed in Great Britain by The Matthews Wright Press, Chard
© compilation and design Duncan Harper
ISBN 0 948975 49 0*